CAMPAIGN • 251

SICILY 1943

The debut of Allied joint operations

STEVEN J ZALOGA   ILLUSTRATED BY HOWARD GERRARD
Series editor Marcus Cowper

First published in Great Britain in 2013 by Osprey Publishing,
PO Box 883, Oxford, OX1 9PL, UK
PO Box 3985, New York, NY 10185-3985, USA
Email: info@ospreypublishing.com

Osprey Publishing is part of Bloomsbury Publishing Plc

Transferred to digital print on demand 2017

First published 2013
3rd impression 2015

Printed and bound by Cenveo Worldwide Limited, USA
A CIP catalog record for this book is available from the British Library.

ISBN: 978 1 78096 126 2
eBook ISBN: 978 1 78096 127 9
ePub ISBN: 978 1 78096 128 6

Editorial by Ilios Publishing Ltd, Oxford, UK (www.iliospublishing.com)
Index by Fionbar Lyons
Typeset in Myriad Pro and Sabon
Maps by Bounford.com
3D bird's-eye view by The Black Spot
Battlescene illustrations by Howard Gerrard
Originated by PDQ Media, Bungay, UK

www.ospreypublishing.com

AUTHOR'S NOTE

The author would like to thank Armando Donato for his help with this
book. Thanks also go to the staff of the US Army's Military History Institute
(MHI) at the Army War College at Carlisle Barracks, PA, and the staff of the
US National Archive, College Park, for their kind assistance in the
preparation of this book.

For brevity, the traditional conventions have been used when referring to
units. In the case of US units, 2/30th Infantry refers to 2nd Battalion, 30th
Infantry Regiment. The US Army traditionally uses Arabic numerals for
divisions and smaller independent formations (9th Division, 751st Tank
Battalion); Roman numerals for corps (II Corps), spelled numbers for field
armies (Seventh US Army) and Arabic numerals for army groups (15th Army
Group). British units generally use Arabic numerals for all formations (5th
Division, 30th Corps, 8th Army). In the case of German units, 2./Panzer-
Regiment 7 refers to the 2nd Company, Panzer-Regiment 7; II./Panzer-
Regiment 7 indicates 2nd Battalion, Panzer-Regiment 7. The Italian unit
abbreviation "fant." is for fanteria (infantry).

Another designation worth mentioning is the Italian practice of identifying
gun calibers, which differs from most other European armies. The Italian
style, such as 75/18, identifies the gun caliber first in millimeters (so in this
case, 75mm) and the gun tube length in calibers (so in this case, L/18).

ARTIST'S NOTE

Readers may care to note that the original paintings from which the color
plates in this book were prepared are available for private sale. The
Publishers retain all reproduction copyright whatsoever. All enquiries
should be addressed to:

Howard Gerrard, 11 Oaks Road, Tenterden, Kent, TN30 6RD, UK

The Publishers regret that they can enter into no correspondence upon
this matter.

THE WOODLAND TRUST

Osprey Publishing are supporting the Woodland Trust, the UK's leading
woodland conservation charity, by funding the dedication of trees.

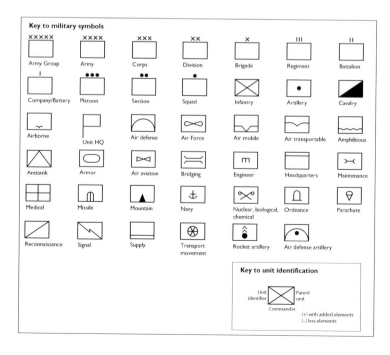

CONTENTS

Axis dispositions on Sicily, July 10, 1943

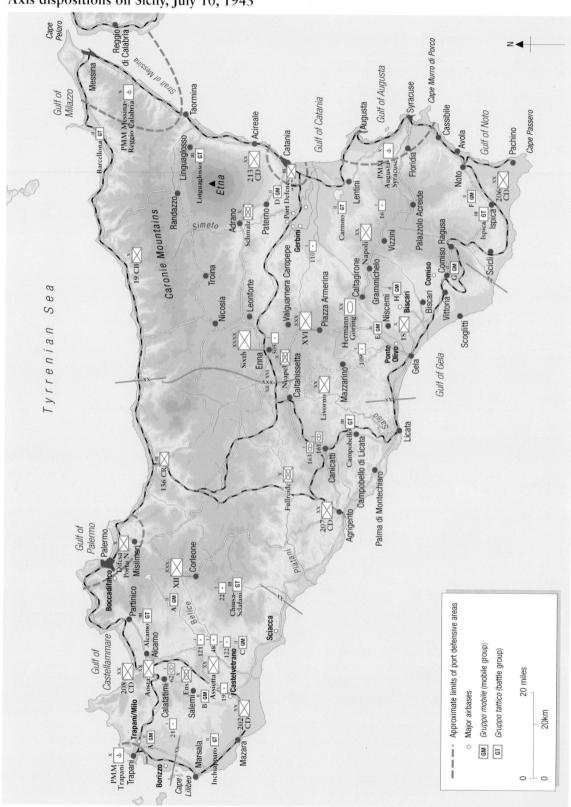

INTRODUCTION

For Germany, the invasion of Sicily on July 10, 1943 marked the turning point of the war. The Wehrmacht was badly overextended on all fronts. This first Allied penetration into "Fortress Europe" threatened to force Italy's withdrawal from the war. The loss of 40 Italian divisions on occupation duty in Greece, Yugoslavia and southern France would oblige the Wehrmacht to replace them with German troops. The impending collapse of Italy prompted Hitler to call off Operation *Zitadelle*, the German offensive against the Kursk salient, on July 13, 1943. Germany lost the strategic initiative in the war and would be on the defensive ever after. Operation *Husky* alone was not responsible for this climactic turn in the fortunes of war. It was merely the culmination of a series of disasters that halted German momentum in 1943.

In spite of its ultimate strategic success, Operation *Husky* was controversial. Much of the early planning for the operation was hasty and slapdash, and there have been enduring arguments that other targets, such as Sardinia, would have been more fruitful objectives. The Allied advance on Sicily was frustrated by a relatively small German force, raising the issue of whether other tactical approaches would have been preferable. Most embarrassing of all, the Germans and Italians managed to evacuate much of their strength across the Messina Straits in spite of Allied naval and aerial superiority. For all the faults of its execution, the Sicilian campaign showed the growing abilities of the Allies in conducting complicated combined operations, a vital tactical skill that would be essential the next summer in Normandy.

The military geography of Sicily is dominated by Mount Etna in eastern Sicily. This active volcano dominates the approaches to Messina, and this is a view of from the southwest in the area traversed by the British 13th Corps during the 1943 campaign. (US Navy)

THE STRATEGIC SITUATION

The first few months of 1943 were a disaster for Germany, but even more so for Italy. Stalingrad was a well-known German defeat, but it is often forgotten that Italy's forces in Russia were dealt a severe blow. The Italian 8ª Armata ARMIR (Armata Italiana in Russia) lost 85,000 troops, with 20,000 dead and 64,000 captured. Further amplifying this catastrophe was the defeat of the Axis in Tunisia, which struck Italy far more severely than Germany.

The Allied victory in Tunisia in May 1943 opened the possibility of taking the war directly to Italian shores. Churchill was convinced that in the wake of the defeat of the Italian army in North Africa, a successful operation on Italian soil would knock Italy out of the war. Rome's defection from the Axis camp would impact on the Wehrmacht as well. Of Italy's 85 divisions, about half were stationed in Russia or the Balkans. While they were not equivalent to the German divisions in combat power, their sudden disappearance would force the Wehrmacht to move forces from other sectors to maintain the occupation in Greece and Yugoslavia.

Allied planning for a summer campaign began prior to the Tunisian victory, with a variety of objectives under consideration. The most obvious choices were Sardinia or Sicily. Sardinia was the more attractive of the two options if the Allied strategic plans anticipated an eventual invasion of the Italian mainland. The capture of Sardinia would place Allied forces opposite central Italy, threatening Rome itself. Sardinia would also place the Allies in easy reach of Corsica, a stepping stone into southern France or Italy's industrialized north. In spite of these attractions, Sardinia posed a significant tactical problem for the Allies since such an operation would have to be conducted beyond the range of Allied land-based fighters. The Axis had demonstrated considerable skill over the past two years of war in the Mediterranean in frustrating Allied naval operations using land-based aircraft and, without the counterweight of Allied fighters, this threat dampened the appeal of Sardinia as the objective in 1943. Sicily was the other obvious choice in the Mediterranean and its southern beaches were within range of airbases on Malta.

The decision to attack Sicily was made in January 1943 at the Casablanca conference. The American Joint Chiefs of Staff under Gen. George C. Marshall had made clear their preference for a cross-Channel attack into northern France in 1943. The British chiefs under Field Marshal Sir Alan Brooke contended that such an operation was premature until Allied forces were stronger. He forcefully argued that continued Allied operations in the Mediterranean were more feasible, would maintain the momentum in the region, and would force the Wehrmacht to divert additional divisions to this theater, thereby weakening defenses in northern France. Both sides agreed that some large operation would be needed to placate the Russians, who were bearing the brunt of the land war against Germany. In the end, Marshall agreed to continue operations in the Mediterranean in the summer of 1943 provided that they did not require the diversion of troops earmarked for the future cross-Channel operation. Since the US side would not commit to further operations in Italy after the summer 1943 landings, Sicily was the prudent choice, and a decision was reached on January 18, 1943. General Dwight Eisenhower was appointed to head the Allied Forces Headquarters (AFHQ) for the campaign.

ALLIED PREPARATIONS: OPERATION *CORKSCREW*

The Italian islands on the approaches to Sicily had been an aggravation to Allied operations in the Mediterranean through 1943. Mussolini had fortified the island of Pantelleria since the late 1930s as an Italian counterweight to the British garrison on nearby Malta. Italian propaganda trumpeted Pantelleria as the "Italian Gibraltar." During the North African and Malta campaigns of 1940–43, the island had been a major airbase for German and Italian aircraft and its location midway between Tunisia and Sicily made it an ideal sentry to guard against the approach of an Allied invasion fleet heading to Sicily.

The Italian military garrison under Ammiraglio Gino Pavesi was 10,600 men, with a slightly larger civilian population. An assault on the island was opposed by the Allied army commander, Gen Harold Alexander, who pointed out that the island was ringed with rocky cliffs, with only a single plausible landing beach that was heavily defended. Nevertheless, Eisenhower wanted the island captured along with the smaller islands of the Pelagie group, including Lampedusa, as a prelude to any operation against Sicily. Radars on the island could track any Allied convoys heading to Sicily and the air and naval bases on the island continued to harass Allied convoys. Capture of the airfields on Pantelleria would also provide the Allies with extra airbase capacity closer to Sicily, and Malta was already overcrowded.

Operation *Corkscrew* depended on a massive aerial assault on the island to break the will of the garrison as a prelude to any landing. The bulk of the attacks were carried out by Lt. Gen. Carl Spaatz's North African Strategic Air Force (NASAF), which included four B-17 heavy bomber groups and five medium bomber groups, along with escort fighters. The campaign began on May 18 with daily medium bomber attacks, followed on June 1 by B-17 raids. By the end of the first phase of *Corkscrew* on June 6, NASAF had conducted more than 1,700 sorties and dropped 1,300 tons of bombs on the

Operation *Corkscrew* was aimed at eliminating the threat posed by the fortified island of Pantellaria. The port area seen here was subjected to intense aerial bombardment during the final phase of the Allied bombardment from June 7 to June 11. (NARA)

small island. The final phase of the air assault took place from June 7 until the scheduled assault landing on June 11, totaling a further 5,325 tons of bombs and 3,710 sorties. The air attacks were conducted around the clock with a special focus on coastal batteries. Starting on June 8, the Royal Navy began a bombardment from offshore. Surrender demands went unanswered so, on the night of June 10–11, the British 1st Division debarked from North Africa for an amphibious assault.

As the Allied planners had hoped, the air attacks had severely demoralized both the civilian and military populations of the island. As disheartening as the bombardment was Rome's refusal to send any aid, the island was expected to fight to the last without hope of reinforcement. On June 2, Pavesi informed Rome that the situation was hopeless and it was only a matter of time before the island was forced to capitulate. On the evening of June 10, before the arrival of the Allied amphibious force, Pavesi informed Rome that the island's capacity to resist was practically finished. On the morning of June 11, Pavesi reported to the Supermarina, Italian Navy high command, that he would request surrender terms. The first Royal Navy warships appeared through the smoke around 1000hrs on July 11, but the landings waited until the smoke cleared. There was some minor firing as British landing craft approached the port, but the island surrendered without any significant fighting. Lampedusa and two small islands surrendered on June 12. The Allied seizure of the islands convinced Axis tactical commanders that Sicily was probably the next objective, but Rome continued to believe that Sardinia was next, and Berlin was convinced that Greece and Sardinia remained the targets.

ALLIED PREPARATIONS: AIR SUPERIORITY

One of the main Allied concerns for the Operation *Husky* landings was the threat posed by Axis airpower. The capabilities of land-based bombers and torpedo aircraft against maritime targets had been demonstrated time and time again in the 1941–43 Mediterranean fighting, and there was considerable anxiety over the vulnerability of the Allied landing fleets once they approached the shores of Sicily. In April 1943, Allied intelligence estimated that there would be 840 German and 1,100 Italian aircraft in the Sicily–Sardinia–Pantelleria region and that the landings would face attack by 545 German and 250 Italian aircraft. Intelligence assessments painted a grim picture of likely Allied losses, suggesting that as many as 300 ships were likely to be sunk. To preempt the Axis air threat, an air campaign against the Axis airfields was initiated in May 1943. Additional resources for these attacks came from a heavy influx of US Army Air Force (USAAF) bombers, including the diversion of B-17 heavy bomber groups that had originally been earmarked for strategic bombing missions out of Britain.

The first wave of air attacks in May 1943 was directed against airbases on Sicily and Sardinia and, through the course of the month, other major concentrations on the Italian mainland were also struck. Airbases in Greece were attacked to mask the actual objective of Sicily, as well as to maximize the attrition of the Luftwaffe's forces in the Mediterranean in general. Besides the airfield attacks, other targets were struck, including the docks and ferry crossings on the Messina Straits that fed reinforcements to Sicily from the Italian mainland. The *Husky* plan called for a concentration on Sicilian

Allied planning was heavily influenced by early intelligence forecasts, which suggested potentially catastrophic casualties from Axis air attacks. One of the prime culprits was the German medium bomber force based on Sicily and in neighboring areas of Italy, such as this Ju-88 of KG30, which was based in the shadows of Mount Etna in the Catania area at the various Gerbini airfields. (NARA)

targets starting on D-8 (July 2) with a substantial intensification on all Axis airbases in range of the island. These were conducted by day with USAAF B-17 and B-24 bombers and at night by RAF Wellingtons. The Luftwaffe responded at first by trying to shift operations to satellite fields constructed near the main airbases, but these were repeatedly struck as well. The main Sicilian airbase at Gerbini, along with its 12 satellite airstrips, were largely unserviceable by the time of the invasion and, of the 19 main Sicilian airbases, all but Sciacca and Trapani were severely damaged or abandoned. About three-quarters of Allied pre-invasion airstrikes were directed against Axis airbases, totaling some 3,000 tons of bombs. The Luftwaffe was forced to withdraw its bomber and fighter-bomber groups from Sicily by the second week of July. Total Axis aircraft losses on the ground during the bombing campaign were 227 aircraft destroyed and 183 damaged, including 113 destroyed and 119 damaged on Sicily.

Malta provided an invaluable staging area for Operation *Husky* and served as the base for most air operations by RAF units. Wellington squadrons based on Malta were the primary night bombing force during the campaign. Here, a Universal Carrier is used as an impromptu tractor to tow bombs out to a Wellington during muddy weather. (NARA)

CHRONOLOGY

January 18, 1943	Allied commanders approve plan to land on Sicily after victory in Tunisia.
March 15	First "Tactical Appreciation" plan for Operation *Husky* completed.
May 9–13	Surrender of Axis forces in Tunisia.
May 18	Operation *Corkscrew* begins the attack on the fortified island of Pantelleria.
May 19	Plan for Operation *Husky* approved.
June 11	Pantelleria surrenders and is occupied by Allied forces.
July 2	Allied air forces initiate preparatory air campaign against Sicily.
July 9	Allied naval force departs Malta and North African ports for Sicily.
July 10	Allied forces begin Operation *Husky* with airborne landings; amphibious landings begin before dawn.
July 11	Axis counterattacks continue with major assaults at Gela, Licata, and Floridia.
July 13	In response to Operation *Husky* Hitler calls off Operation *Zitadelle*, the Kursk offensive on the Russian Front.
July 13	Montgomery decides to change plans for reduction of Sicily with a 30th Corps advance northwest of Mount Etna.
July 13	At 2200hrs, No. 3 Commando lands and seizes Melati bridge; bridge lost the next day.
July 14	In the pre-dawn hours, 1st Parachute Brigade conducts Operation *Fustian* to seize Primosole bridge.
July 15	Generalabust Hube arrives on Sicily to establish XIV Panzer Korps headquarters.
July 16	British forces recapture Primosole bridge.

July 17	Alexander agrees to Patton's plan for Seventh US Army to capture Palermo and western Sicily.
July 17	Arisio's 12° Corpo ordered to withdraw into eastern Sicily and take over sector north of Mount Etna.
July 19	The Seventh US Army's Provisional Corps begins its race toward Palermo.
July 22	Palermo surrenders.
July 23	Bradley's II Corps reaches the northern Sicilian coast; Trapani falls to the Provisional Corps.
July 24	Fascist Grand Council agrees to oust Mussolini.
July 25	Mussolini is forced to resign by the king.
July 26	Hitler tentatively agrees to the evacuation of Sicily.
July 29	The British 30th Corps begins Operation *Hardgate* offensive with parallel attack by US II Corps.
August 2	Kesselring approves Operation *Lehrgang* evacuation plan.
August 3	Italian forces begin evacuation of units across the Messina Straits.
August 4	Panzer-Division "Hermann Göring" begins withdrawal from Catania.
August 5	15. Panzergrenadier-Division conducts withdrawal from Troina.
August 8	Kesselring authorizes Hube to start Operation *Lehrgang* evacuation.
August 9	15. Panzergrenadier-Division pulled out of the line to prepare for evacuation.
August 11	Task Force Bernard conducts second amphibious landing at Brolo.
August 11–12	Operation *Lehrgang* starts with the evacuation of 15. Panzer-Division.
August 15–16	29. Panzergrenadier-Division evacuated over Messina Straits.
August 16	A platoon from the US 7th Infantry Regiment enters outskirts of Messina during the evening.
August 16–17	Panzer-Division HG withdraws over Messina Straits; Operation *Lehrgang* completed.
August 17	Patton conducts surrender ceremony in Messina during the late morning.
September 3	Italian government signs secret armistice agreement with the Allies.
September 8	Italian armistice agreement is publicly announced; Italy withdraws from the war.

OPPOSING COMMANDERS

AXIS COMMANDERS

In contrast to the Allies, there was no unified command on the Axis side. Distrust on both sides was reaching poisonous levels by the early summer of 1943, as the Germans suspected that the Italians were on the verge of departing the war. The Italians were resentful of German domination, especially after Rommel's heavy-handed style in North Africa, and feared that Germany planned to occupy Italy. Axis command on Sicily was nominally in Italian hands under the Comando Supremo in Rome, but, in practice, the Germans took control.

The Italian supreme commander had been **Generale d'armata Ugo Cavalerro**, who had enjoyed good relations with the Germans through the desert campaigns. As Mussolini began to have doubts about the Axis alliance, on February 1, 1943, he switched command to **Vittorio Ambrosio**, who loathed the Germans. Ambrosio strongly opposed further offensive operations in Russia and urged Berlin to adopt a defensive posture. This greatly strained relations between the OKW (Oberkommando der Wehrmacht: Armed Forces High Command) and the Comando Supremo. Similar changes in other commands shifted the senior Italian leadership in a decidedly anti-German direction. Mussolini tried to deflect attention from this change by removing his son-in-law, Count Galeazzo Ciano, from leadership of the foreign ministry, because he had been engaged in a variety of intrigues to pull Italy out of the Rome–Berlin alliance and to reach a separate peace with the Allies.

Generale d'armata Alfredo Guzzoni led the Commando Forze Armate della Sicilia in July 1943. The FF.AA. Sicilia headquarters incorporated the army's 6° Armata plus the other subordinate services. (MHI)

Generale d'armata Mario Roatta was appointed commander of 6ª Armata (Sixth Army) on Sicily in February 1943. Roatta had been army chief of staff and he insisted that the dysfunctional command structure on the island be placed under a centralized control. At the time, the army commander did not control the anti-aircraft forces of the Fascist Militia, nor the various paramilitary formations assigned to civilian prefectures. In addition, the navy and air force units on Sicily were under their own commands, and the sizable naval bases on Sicily were under the autonomous command of the Supermarina. On March 28, 1943, a unified command of the various Italian forces was established under Roatta's new Comando Forze Armate della Sicilia (FF.AA. Sicilia: Armed Forces Command Sicily), which also included subordination of German units on the island. Roatta attempted to strengthen the garrison on Sicily, put the island on a war footing, and amplify the fortification program. Nevertheless, his command proved to be short-lived as, in late May 1943, he issued a proclamation that local Sicilian politicians felt impugned local patriotism.

In his place, Mussolini ordered the 66-year-old **Generale d'Armata Alfredo Guzzoni** out of retirement to take over the command of 6ª Armata. Guzzoni had served as a young officer in the Great War and was governor of Eritrea after the Second Italo-Abyssinian War from 1936 to 1937. He commanded Italian forces in Albania and Greece in 1939–40 and led 4ª Armata during the invasion of France in June 1940. In November 1940, Guzzoni was appointed Undersecretary of War and Deputy Chief of the Supreme General Staff before his retirement. Guzzoni had a reputation as a determined and single-minded commander with a strong grasp of strategy. He developed good working relations with the senior German commanders. At least on paper, Guzzoni held command over both Italian and German forces on Sicily. In reality, German tactical commanders often disregarded instructions from Italian sources. In an attempt to improve cooperation, the Wehrmacht established a liaison office with Guzzoni's headquarters, headed by **Generalleutnant Frido von Senger und Etterlin**. A Bavarian Catholic who spoke fluent Italian, Senger und Etterlin had a distinguished military career prior to being sent to Sicily in June 1943 after having received personal instructions from Hitler about this delicate position. Senger und Etterlin is better known for his later command at Monte Cassino.

The Regio Marina had its own autonomous naval command structure on Sicily, headed by **Ammiraglio di squadra Pietro Barone**. Barone's command was primarily responsible for Sicily's large naval bases and the smaller ports. These bases were independent of the army and had their own defense. The Italian air force on Sicily was commanded by **Generale di divisione aerea Adriano Monti,** but his forces withered away in the face of relentless Allied air attacks.

The critical German commander was **Generalfeldmarschall Albert Kesselring,** who served as Oberbefehlshaber Süd (Senior Commander South). In October 1942, Hitler granted Kesselring tactical authority over all German military units in Italy, one of the few times when a theater commander was granted unified command. As a Luftwaffe rather than army officer, Kesselring was an unusual figure in such a senior command post. Nevertheless, his varied career and organizational talents made him an ideal theater commander. Kesselring had begun his military career in the Bavarian artillery, being elevated to the general staff in the winter of 1917. He remained in the Reichswehr until 1933, when he was ordered to become chief administrator of the Air Ministry in civilian mufti. His primary responsibility was the creation of the infrastructure of the new Luftwaffe, and this attracted the favorable attention of the Luftwaffe head, Hermann Göring. By the time war broke out, he had returned to uniform as commander of Luftflotte 1, the tactical close-support bomber and Stuka force that played such a prominent role in the 1939 campaign against Poland and later as commander of Luftflotte 2 during the 1940 campaign against France. Kesselring was appointed to OB-Süd in December 1941 and given the politically challenging task of coordinating the German war effort in North Africa with the Italian armed forces. His political charms led to his nickname of "Smiling Albert." Kesselring was popular in Berlin as he maintained an optimistic facade in spite of the declining Axis fortunes in the Mediterranean;

Generalfeldmarschall Albert Kesselring served as Oberbefehlshaber Süd during the Sicily campaign. He was known as "Smiling Albert" because of his cheerful personality. (Library of Congress)

Hitler was never pleased with naysayers and pessimists. He proved to be an astute and effective operational leader and certainly one of Germany's most insightful strategic commanders during the war.

ALLIED COMMANDERS

The Allied Forces Headquarters was led by **General Dwight Eisenhower**. Ike was a protégé of Gen. George C. Marshall, the chairman of the US Joint Chiefs of Staff and President Roosevelt's primary military adviser. In 1942, Eisenhower was appointed as commander for the forthcoming Operation *Torch* landings in North Africa. This set a precedent of having an American in theater command, while the three subordinates for army, navy, and air force headquarters were all British. Eisenhower displayed exceptional political skills in managing relations between senior British and American commanders in spite of significant differences in strategic viewpoints and different staff cultures. He also proved adept at dealing with senior civilian command authorities and developed a comfortable working relationship with Winston Churchill. Eisenhower often described his role as that of "chairman of the board" rather than warlord. Eisenhower was excessively deferential to senior British commanders in the final stages of the Tunisia campaign and was still attempting to create a workable multinational headquarters when planning began for Operation *Husky*. Most of the planning for the Sicily campaign was undertaken by British organizations. Eisenhower was dismayed when AFHQ followed the British style of "committee" management with each of the three British services having an equal voice in the decision-making process for Sicily instead of the US style of a unified command. Controversies during the Sicily campaign led Eisenhower to insist on a unified command approach when he took over the Supreme Headquarters Allied Expeditionary Force (SHAEF) in 1944 for the Normandy invasion.

The senior Allied land commander was Gen. Sir Harold Alexander, commander of 15th Army Group. (NARA)

The senior Allied land force commander was **General Sir Harold Alexander**. He was a divisional commander in France in 1940 and appointed as a corps commander during the Dunkirk operation; the other corps commander was Bernard Montgomery. He was appointed General Officer Commanding-in-Chief (GOC-in-C) Burma in February 1942, leading the 14th Army from India. In August 1942, Alexander replaced Claude Auchinleck as the Commander-in-Chief of Middle East Command and concurrently, Lieutenant-General Bernard Montgomery took command of the Eighth Army under his direction. Alexander's command became the basis for the new 15th Army Group, which was responsible for the land forces of Operation *Husky*. Alexander was a popular and respected commander and, like Eisenhower, he fostered cooperation between British and American commands in the difficult early stages of their strategic relationship. However, he failed to impose any sort of operational or strategic vision on his subordinate commanders, and his diffident command style left the door open for more aggressive commanders like Montgomery and Patton to push for their own courses of action during the Sicily campaign.

The two Allied field commanders were Gen. Sir Bernard L. Montgomery, commander of the British 8th Army, and Lt. Gen. George S. Patton Jr, commander of the Seventh US Army, seen here on July 26, 1943 at Patton's headquarters near Palermo. (NARA)

Bernard Law Montgomery took command of the dispirited 8th Army in 1942, leading it on a string of victories starting with the El Alamein. His record of success in North Africa gave him considerable influence in the planning and execution of Operation *Husky*. Montgomery's counterpart on the American side was **George Patton**. He headed the Western Task Force during the Operation *Torch* landings in French North Africa in November 1942 and his I Armored Corps performed garrison duty in Algeria. After the Kasserine Pass debacle in February 1943, he took command of II Corps in Tunisia, helping to rejuvenate the inexperienced and poorly led US forces in the 1943 spring offensives. He was pulled out of II Corps command shortly before the conclusion of the Tunisian campaign in order to prepare the Seventh US Army for *Husky*.

The two senior Allied naval commanders were the Royal Navy's Admiral Sir Andrew Cunningham to the right and the US Navy's Rear Admiral H. Kent Hewitt to the left, seen here aboard the command ship USS *Ancon* in September 1943. (NARA)

The senior Allied air commanders were the RAF's Air Chief Marshal Sir Arthur Tedder (left) and US Army Air Force Lt. Gen. Carl Spaatz (right). (NARA)

Major-General G. G. Simonds, commander of 1st Canadian Infantry Division, comes ashore at Bark South beach on July 10, 1943. Simonds later commanded II Canadian Corps in Normandy. (NARA)

The senior naval command for Operation *Husky* was the Royal Navy's **Admiral Andrew Cunningham**. He headed the Royal Navy's Mediterranean Fleet in 1943 and was appointed Supreme Commander, Allied Expeditionary Forces for Operation *Husky*. He served most of his career in the Mediterranean, starting in the Great War. Cunningham won fame in a series of devastating victories over the Italian fleet, including Taranto in November 1940 and Cape Matapan in March 1941. His intimate knowledge of the heavy price paid in the fight with Turkish coastal defenses in the Dardanelles in 1915 helps to explain the Royal Navy's lack of enthusiasm in tangling with Italian defenses in the Messina Straits in August 1943.

The senior air command was **Air Chief Marshal Sir Arthur Tedder**. He was appointed Air Officer Commander-in-Chief, RAF Middle East Command in June 1941 and commanded the Desert Air Force during the entire North African campaign. As the most experienced Middle East air commander, he led the Allied Air Forces during Operation *Husky*. He greatly impressed Eisenhower both with his technical knowledge and his astute political skills, and Tedder became Deputy Supreme Commander Allied Expeditionary Force (SHAEF) for the European campaign in 1944–45.

OPPOSING FORCES

AXIS FORCES

Italian Army

The coast of Sicily had been fortified since ancient times and there had been repeated efforts to modernize the defenses over the previous half-century. Between 1884 and 1914, the Umbertini Forts were built to cover the Messina Straits, consisting of 13 fortified batteries on the Sicilian side and nine on the Calabrian coast. This was followed by an extensive coast defense program during World War I so that, by 1918, the Sicilian coast was covered by 92 gun batteries, including 192 guns. The most impressive of these was the Batteria Opera A on Cape Santa Panagia, equipped with twin 15in. Vickers guns in a battleship turret with fortified magazines. This battery covered the approaches to the posts of Syracuse and Augusta. At the time of the 1943 fighting, the Milmart (Milizia Artiglieria Marittima) on Sicily included 58 anti-ship gun batteries and 241 dual role (anti-aircraft/anti-ship) batteries with about 1,400 weapons.

Italian doctrine until 1943 considered that major ports would be the primary objective of any large-scale amphibious operation. As a result, the major Sicilian ports had their own naval base commands (PMM: Piazza Militare Marittime) with their own defense forces, including coastal infantry

The Italian coastal divisions on Sicily were heavily dependent on captured equipment and war booty provided from Germany. This Italian infantryman is operating the modified Greek version of the Hotchkiss M.1926 6.5mm light machine gun. (MHI)

17

battalions, coastal antiship gun batteries, antiaircraft batteries, and artillery trains. There were three of these defense commands on Sicily, PMM Messina-Reggio Calabria, PMM Augusta-Siracusa, and PMM Trapani. Two other ports received more modest defensive works, Difesa Porto E (Est: Catania) and Difesa Porto N (Nord: Palermo), and their defenses were under regional army control.

Before the war, Italian army doctrine viewed open coastlines as unlikely objectives in a large-scale amphibious assault owing to the requirement for ports for supply needs. As a result, coastal defense away from the ports was weak through 1941. Italian doctrine began to change because of the British Commando raiding. A program to fortify the coastline between the ports was started in 1941 with Sicily and Sardinia receiving priority. However, the program was undermined by shortages of concrete and other supplies. Nevertheless, several hundred pillboxes and fortified positions were completed on Sicily in 1942–43 prior to the landings. To man the new defenses, the first coastal brigades (*Brigate costiere*) were organized in 1941, followed by coastal divisions (*Divisione costiere*) in 1942. By 1943, a total of 25 coastal divisions had been formed, of which five divisions and two brigades were located on Sicily.

The coastal divisions were the weakest Italian formations on Sicily. They were raised from local recruits with a smattering of regular army personnel and were poorly trained, weakly armed, and immobile. They were usually equipped with war-booty equipment from France, Yugoslavia, and Greece. The units were thinly stretched along the coast, with an average of only 26 troops per kilometer and only one antitank gun per 8km of coastline. Their main role was to deal with the threat of commando raids, not a full-scale invasion. In early 1943, the Italians and Germans began to discuss anti-invasion doctrine in light of the British–Canadian landings at Dieppe in August 1942 and the American landings in French North Africa in November 1942. In both cases, the landings had focused on the seizure of ports to

The 47mm A5 vz. 36 gun was manufactured by Skoda in Czechoslovakia for the Yugoslav army and some 821 were absorbed into the Italian army after the 1941 conflict as the Cannone contracarri 47mm M.38 antitank gun. This one was deployed for beach defense near Gela by 429° Battaglione. (NARA)

unload heavy equipment and supplies, but nevertheless it was alarmingly clear that the Allies were experimenting with amphibious tactics suitable for landing heavy equipment, including tanks on open beaches without docks. The Wehrmacht was already embarking on its grandiose Atlantikwall fortification program, and Italian teams were invited to tour strongpoints on the French coast in early 1943. Although impressed by the fortified positions, the Italian army realized it did not have the resources or time to construct such an elaborate defensive position on its extended coastline. As a result, the Comando Supremo in early 1943 authorized a major acceleration of the coastal fortification effort with top priority going to the most likely invasion areas. Since Rome felt that Sardinia was the most likely Allied invasion site, about 1,800 pillboxes were built there. Construction work also increased on Sicily, as well as the neighboring Calabrian coast. Besides the reinforcements along the coast, Italian doctrine began to focus on the threat of airborne assaults. Ninety-six special anti-paratrooper units (NAP: *Nuclei antiparacadutisti*) were formed, usually consisting of a platoon of truck-mounted infantry. These were deployed to shield high-value military positions such as major coastal gun batteries and airbases.

There were a total of 252,000 Italian military personnel on Sicily in July 1943, of whom about 192,000 were in the army. Italian army formations on Sicily were under the command of two corps, XII Corpo in the west and XVI Corpo in the east. Besides the coastal divisions under their command, there were four regular infantry divisions on Sicily. Of these, the Divisione Livorno was significantly larger and better equipped than the other three, with about 14,000 troops versus 11,000 in the other divisions, 600 vehicles versus 12, and 234 machine guns versus 136. This division had been reorganized for use in the planned invasion of Malta. Although it was inexperienced and without adequate training, it was widely regarded as the best Italian unit on Sicily. The division was under army reserve as its primary counterattack force.

The best Italian armored vehicle on Sicily was the Semovente 90/53, which combined the 90mm anti-aircraft gun on the M14/41 tank chassis to create a tank-destroyer. The X Ragguppamento Semoventi had two-dozen of these organized into three independent groups. This was one of five of these vehicles of the 163° Gruppo lost during the fighting near Campobello-Cancatti on July 11–12. (NARA)

Owing to the heavy losses in North Africa, the Italian army on Sicily had no armored divisions. Tank strength totaled 148 and consisted of two battalions, with about a hundred war-booty French Renault R-35 infantry tanks, two separate companies of obsolete Fiat 3000 light tanks, and some scattered units with obsolete L.3 tankettes. There were 68 Semovente assault guns consisting of four partial battalions of Semovente 47/32 light assault guns, a newly arrived company of Semovente 75/18 medium assault guns, and 24 of the new Semovente 90/53 tank destroyers. There were a number of cavalry squadrons with the AB.41 armored car.

The immobility of most of the Italian infantry divisions and the poverty of Italian tank strength convinced Roatta to concentrate his meager armored formations into mobile groups (*Gruppi mobili*) to serve as counterattack forces for anti-invasion defense. They were located near airbases to provide security against paratroop attack. They typically consisted of a company of tanks and a company of towed antitank guns, as well as companies of infantry, motorcycle troops, and artillery depending on what was available. Seven of these were formed, Gruppi Mobili A through C with XII Corpo in western Sicily and Gruppi Mobili E through H with XVI Corpo in eastern Sicily. These mobile units were strong in firepower and mobility but weak in infantry so, at the same time, the complementary battlegroups (*Gruppi tattici*) were created as infantry counterattack forces. These typically consisted of Bersaglieri or other elite light infantry battalions. Each of the corps had four of these battlegroups.

One of Mussolini's favorite slogans was "Believe, obey, fight!" The problem was that many of the Italian troops on Sicily had long since lost faith in the Fascist dream of imperial glory and so were no longer willing to fight. The coastal divisions, recruited mostly from Sicilians with family on the island, had the poorest morale. The regular infantry divisions and combat formations raised in metropolitan Italy had better morale. Officers of the Divisione Livorno felt that morale in their unit was high; this was manifest in their spirited combat performance early in the campaign. The Germans singled out the Italian artillery units for their contribution to the fighting.

AXIS GROUND FORCES, SICILY, JULY 10, 1943

6ª Armata	**Generale d'armata Alfredo Guzzoni**
Army reserve	
Divisione Livorno	Generale divisione Domenico Chirieleison
15. Panzergrenadier-Division	Generalmajor Eberhard Rodt
Panzer-Division "Hermann Göring"	Generalleutnant Paul Conrath
XII Corpo d'armata	**Generale di corpo Mario Arisio**
Divisione Aosta	Generale divisione Giacomo Romano
Divisione Assieta	Generale divisione Erberto Papini
208ª Divisione costiera	Generale divisione Giovanni Marciani
202° Divisione costiera	Generale brigati Gino Ficalbi
207° Divisione costiera	Generale divisione Ottorino Schreiber
Difesa Porto N	Generale brigati Giuseppe Molinero
XVI Corpo d'armata	**Generale di corpo Carlo Rossi**
Divisione Napoli	Generale divisione Giulio Porcinari
213ª Divisione costiera	Generale divisione Carlo Gotti
206° Divisione costiera	Generale divisione Achille d'Havet
XVIII Brigata costiera	Generale brigati Orazio Mariscalco

XIX Brigata costiera	Generale brigati Giovanni Bocchetti
Difesa Porto E	Generale brigati Azzo Passalacqua
Comando Militare Autonomo della Marina di Sicilia	**Ammiraglio di squadra Pietro Barone**
Piazza Militare Marittima Messina-Reggio Calabria	Ammiraglio di squadra Pietro Barone
Piazza Militare Marittima Augusta-Siracusa	Contraammiraglio Priamo Leonardi
Piazza Militare Marittima di Trapani	Contraammiraglio Giuseppe Manfredi

Wehrmacht

The German Army (Heer) used Sicily as a staging area for the Tunisian front through the spring of 1943, and there were no units permanently stationed for its defense until summer. Oberst Ernst-Günther Baade had headed a replacement depot on the island since April 1943, which amalgamated march battalions and other replacement units before dispatching them to Tunisia. An inspired leader, if somewhat eccentric, he had previously been a regimental commander in 15. Panzer-Division in North Africa. With the collapse of the Tunisian front inevitable, in May 1943 Baade began to halt troop shipments to Tunis as an unconscionable waste. He combined the assorted replacement units into the improvised Panzergrenadier-Regiment Palermo, later renamed Regiment Körner. By combining various German Luftwaffe and army support formations on Sicily, Baade was able to create two more units, Regiment Ens and Regiment Fullreide. The formations were eventually relabeled as Division Sizilien and, at the beginning of June, command was taken over by Generalleutnant Eberhard Rodt. The unit was formally redesignated as 15. Panzergrenadier-Division in July 1943, named after the 15. Panzer-Division that had been lost in Tunisia. In spite of its name, it had few armored half-tracks and its tank component was modest, with seven PzKpfw II and 46 PzKpfw IV tanks. Regardless of its motley origins, it had a hard core of experienced veterans and was the better of the two German divisions on Sicily in July 1943.

The most imposing tank force to appear on Sicily was 2. Kompanie, schwere Panzer-Abteilung 504 equipped with the Tiger I heavy tank. This particular tank was captured intact by 505th Parachute Infantry on the Biscari (Agate) road near Biazza ridge on July 11, when its crew was killed outside the tank by a grenade thrown by Lt. Harold Swingler. The Tiger company lost ten of its 17 tanks in the first three days of fighting. (NARA)

In May 1943, Mussolini and Ambrosio agreed to Hitler's offer of three German divisions for the defense of Sicily and Sardinia, so long as they remained under Italian operational control; they refused to accept two more divisions for defense on the mainland owing to Ambrosio's concern that they were Trojan horses and part of a German scheme to dominate Italy. The second Wehrmacht unit earmarked for Sicily was a Luftwaffe division, the Panzer-Division "Hermann Göring". This was the latest incarnation of a string of Göring's pet units. By the time of the 1940 campaign in France the unit had expanded to a motorized flak regiment and it saw extensive combat on the Russian Front in 1941–42, especially notable for its antitank activities. It was raised to divisional size in late 1942 by absorbing Luftwaffe paratroopers, but the embryonic Kampfgruppe Hermann Göring was destroyed in the Tunisian campaign. The remnants of the destroyed division still in Italy were used to reconstitute the Panzer-Division HG and, in late June, Kesselring ordered the incomplete unit to be sent to Sicily. At the time of the Allied invasion, the division had only one complete Panzergrenadier regiment, with only about three battalions worth of infantry, and a Panzer regiment with 53 PzKpfw IIIs, 32 PzKpfw IVs, and 20 StuG III assault guns. A separate company of 17 Tiger tanks was attached to the division. Although favored by the Luftwaffe in terms of supplies and personnel, the division was incomplete, poorly trained in combined arms, and its sub-units were poorly integrated. Kesselring's main concern about the division was its poor leadership. The division was commanded by Generalleutnant Paul Conrath, who had served as a junior artillery officer in World War I and as a police officer through the mid-1930s before he entered the Luftwaffe Flak service. Although he saw considerable combat on the Eastern Front in command of Flak-Regiment HG, he had no real experience or training to lead a Panzer division. Regimental command was even weaker; the division's Panzer regiment was commanded by a former bomber pilot, who had been grounded due to nervous problems. The one bright spot in the division's leadership was Oberst Wilhelm Schmalz, an army infantry officer and Knight's Cross winner who had been attached to the division as an instructor and adviser. He commanded the division's *Kampfgruppe* in the critical Catania sector.

The predominant German tank type on Sicily was the PzKpfw IV, which by this stage of the war, was the backbone of the Panzer force. This particular tank is a PzKpfw IV Ausf. D that has been brought up to later standards by the addition of appliqué armor on the hull and the substitution of the newer and more powerful KwK 40 gun. (NARA)

Axis reconnaissance aircraft played a major role in intelligence gathering prior to the Allied amphibious landings. The Cant Z506B of the 287 Squadriglia RM was based on Sardinia, but often forward deployed to ports on the Sicilian coasts to conduct maritime reconnaissance against Allied shipping. (NARA)

Besides these two divisions, there were a variety of smaller German units on Sicily, most notably Luftwaffe Flak units. The most powerful of these were eight 88mm batteries with mixed Italian and German crews, deployed mainly on the Messina Straits. Total German strength on Sicily in July 1943 was about 67,500 military personnel.

Axis airpower

Axis airpower in the Mediterranean was waning. The Luftwaffe had lost nearly 900 single-engine fighters in the Mediterranean theater in the first half of 1943, and overall had lost 2,422 aircraft in the Tunisian cauldron. The final stages of the North African campaign had dealt an even heavier blow to the Regia Aeronautica, which lost 2,190 aircraft from November 1942 to June 1943. As a consequence, Axis air operations over the Mediterranean in the early summer of 1943, especially anti-shipping missions, did little to hinder Allied preparations.

Immediately prior to the *Husky* landings, the Regia Aeronautica had a total of 930 combat aircraft in Italy, but only 449 were serviceable. Of these, about 620 were in central and southern Italy in range of Sicily. The Regia Aeronautica on Sicily had 15 fighter squadrons, two observation squadrons, four maritime reconnaissance flights, and one torpedo squadron. Although the paper strength of this force was impressive, actual air strength on Sicily was modest owing to chronic shortage of spare parts, which left a portion of Italian aircraft immobile, exacerbated by the heavy combat losses from Allied pre-invasion bombardment. At the time of the invasion, there were about 140 fighters, 80 fighter-bombers, and 35 bombers operating from Sicilian airfields, of which only about 80 were operational. These were reinforced by 210 operational warplanes at neighboring airbases in Calabria, Corsica, and Sardinia.

Sicily had been a major center of Luftwaffe air operations in 1941–43, under the direction of Luftflotte 2 (2nd Air Fleet). More than 400 aircraft were sent to reinforce the Mediterranean theater from France and the Russian front, but attrition ate up most of the gains. In early July 1943, the air fleet had an official strength of 667 warplanes, although its actual operational strength was only 443 aircraft. Its offensive force was based around six Ju-88 bomber groups, two weak He-111 torpedo-bomber groups, three fast bomber groups of Me-110 and Me-210, and several strike groups with Ju-87 Stuka or FW-190 fighter-bombers. The bomber force had played a critical role in Luftwaffe anti-shipping operations in 1941–43, as well as the campaign against Malta. The defensive force included four Bf-109 fighter groups and a single Ju-88 night fighter group. One of the most important elements of Luftflotte 2 was its reconnaissance arm, consisting of a group of Ju-88s, a group of radar-equipped He-11s, and a long-range Bf-109 photo group. Axis intelligence relied on this force and their Italian counterparts to keep track of Allied invasion shipping.

Much of Luftflotte 2 had been based on Pantelleria and Sicily during the earlier Mediterranean campaigns, but the Allied air attacks forced the withdrawal of bomber units in favor of safer bases in southern France and Italy. This significantly diminished the striking power of the Luftwaffe in the subsequent campaign. Luftwaffe fighter strength on the island fell from about 185 fighters on July 3, when the Allied pre-invasion air assault began, to only about 100 fighters by the time of the landings a week later; the fighter-bomber force numbered 80 but they were evacuated. The fighter force was withdrawn to nearby bases in neighboring Calabria, Sardinia, or the Naples area, which placed them within range of Sicily, but with much diminished endurance over the invasion beaches.

Axis naval power

The Italian navy had been badly battered by the previous fighting in the Mediterranean. By the summer of 1943, it had lost 13 cruisers and 36 destroyers; ten cruisers and 20 destroyers remained but many were laid up for repairs. Almost as debilitating was the severe shortage of fuel, which constrained Italian naval operations; Italy was almost entirely dependent on Germany for fuel. Allied naval commanders were concerned by the threat of the larger Italian capital ships, especially the three new battleships of the Littorio class should they make a sortie against the invasion force. However, the Supermarina viewed them as a "fleet-in-being" rather than risk them to Allied air and naval attack. Most Italian naval activity during Operation *Husky* involved submarines or light coastal forces. By the time of the *Husky* landings, the Kriegsmarine surface forces had only a minor presence in Italian waters, mainly supply and support vessels. In the face of ferocious Allied anti-submarine forces, the small Axis submarine force proved ineffective and lost three U-boats and nine Italian submarines in July.

Allied naval planners were deeply worried about the threat posed by Italian capital ships and, in particular, by its three modern Vittorio Veneto-class battleships like the *Littorio* seen here. In the event, Rome decided against risking the battleships and they saw no fighting during the Sicily campaign. (NARA)

ALLIED FORCES

British Army

The 8th Army invasion force consisted of two corps, with 13th Corps landing in the Gulf of Noto with 50th Division and 5th Division and 30th Corps landing on the Pachino peninsula with the Canadian 1st Division and 51st Division. All three British divisions had extensive combat experience in 1940–43. The Canadian 1st Infantry Division had been mobilized in 1939 and dispatched to Britain, where it trained for nearly three years before departing for Operation *Husky*. The 8th Army did not deploy an armored division on Sicily since the terrain was not felt to be suited to large-scale mechanized operations. Instead, each corps had an armored brigade for support, 4th Armoured Brigade with 13th Corps and 23rd Armoured Brigade with 30th Corps. The army reserve included 78th Infantry Division and the Canadian 1st Army Tank Brigade.

Besides the divisional formations, a number of special forces units played a role in invasion plans. Units of the British 1st Airborne Division were allotted to Operation *Husky*, with 1st Air-Landing Brigade assigned to seize the Ponte Grande bridge at the outset of the operation and 1st Parachute Brigade being held in reserve for follow-on missions. Several other battalion-sized special forces units were assigned missions during the amphibious assault, including No. 3 Commando, 1st Special Raiding Squadron (SAS), and No. 40 and No. 41 Royal Marine Commandos.

A 25-pdr crew of 51st Highland Division fires on German positions during the fighting in the foothills of Mount Etna in August 1943. (NARA)

A pair of Sherman III tanks of the Canadian 1st Army Tank Brigade on a dust-clogged road that supported 13th Corps. (NARA)

The Free French contribution to the Allied forces fighting on Sicily was the 4e Tabor of Moroccan Goums, the legendary colonial mountain troops. This unit served as part of the Seventh US Army, usually alongside 1st Division. (NARA)

8th Army	**General Sir Bernard L. Montgomery**
1st Airborne Division	Major-General G. F. Hopkinson
13th Corps	**Lieutenant-General Miles Dempsey**
5th Division	Major-General G. C. Bucknall
50th Northumbrian Division	Major-General Sidney Kirkman
30th Corps	**Lieutenant-General Oliver Leese**
51st Highland Division	Major-General Douglas Wimberly
1st Canadian Division	Major-General G. G. Simonds

US Army

Patton's Seventh US Army entered the Sicily campaign with only a single corps headquarters, Bradley's II Corps. Patton's previous command, I Armored Corps headquarters, had been used to create the new Seventh US Army headquarters. This proved awkward in practice, and Patton subsequently added a Provisional Corps headquarters under his deputy, Maj. Gen. Geoffrey Keyes, to create a more typical command structure.

As in the case of British 8th Army, Patton's Seventh US Army drew most of its units from the two corps that had taken part in the North African campaign. The original plans called for the landing of the inexperienced 36th Division, but Patton wanted a proven unit to land in the critical Gela sector and so the "Big Red One" was substituted. Both the 1st and 9th Infantry Divisions had fought in Tunisia. The 3rd Infantry Division and 2nd Armored Division took part in the initial landings in French North Africa but not in the subsequent fighting in Tunisia. The 82nd Airborne Division arrived in North Africa in May 1943, immediately prior to Operation *Husky*, and 45th Division departed for Sicily from the United States. The US Army deployed a larger armored contingent on Sicily than the British, not only 2nd Armored Division, but also two separate tank battalions that were attached to II Corps for infantry support. The US also deployed its special forces to the Sicily operation, the 1st and 4th Rangers with Darby's Force X.

Seventh US Army	**Lieutenant-General George S Patton**
2nd Armored Division	Major-General Ernie Harmon
3rd Infantry Division	Major-General Lucian Truscott
9th Infantry Division	Major-General Manton Eddy
82nd Airborne Division	Major-General Matthew Ridgway
II Corps	**Lieutenant-General Omar Bradley**
1st Infantry Division	Major-General Terry Allen
45th Division	Major-General Troy Middleton

Allied air forces

Allied Air Forces were under a unified command, the Mediterranean Air Command (MAC), headed by RAF Air Chief Marshal Sir Arthur Tedder. The main components were the Northwest African Air Force (NAAF), headed by USAAF Lt. Gen. Carl Spaatz, and the Middle East Air Command (MEAC), under RAF Air Chief Marshal Douglas, along with the subsidiary Malta Air Command. The NAAF's main deep strike force was Northwest African Strategic Air Force (NASAF), commanded by Maj. Gen. James Doolittle, and this consisted of the USAAF bombers of XII Bomber Command and four wings of RAF Wellington night bombers. The tactical forces oriented toward the ground support mission were directed by Air Vice Marshal Sir Arthur Coningham's North African Tactical Air Force. This included the RAF's Desert Air Force, the USAAF's XII Air Support Group, and the Tactical Bomber Force. Major-General Lewis Brereton's Ninth Air Force had its fighter and medium bomber groups subordinated to MEAC while its five B-24 heavy bomber groups remained under its own headquarters, owing to the forthcoming raid on the Ploesti oil facilities. Besides these substantial forces, the Northwest African Coastal Air Force, under Air Marshal Sir Hugh Lloyd, was responsible for air defense of Allied airbases, maritime reconnaissance, anti-submarine operations, and shipping strikes. In total, the Allied air forces deployed about 1,670 combat aircraft, plus 835 reconnaissance, transport, and support aircraft, in a total of 146 US and 121 British squadrons. This was substantially larger than the Axis air forces in the region.

Allied fighters began operating off airbases on Sicily within days of the landings. In the foreground is a P-40 Warhawk of 33rd Fighter Group, while behind are a pair of A-36 Invaders taking off from Licata. Two fighter-bomber groups operated the A-36 on Sicily, 27th and 86th FBG. (NARA)

Allied navies

Operation *Husky* was the largest amphibious landing in history up to that date. Admiral Andrew Cunningham's Allied Expeditionary Forces consisted of two main elements, Admiral Sir Bertram Ramsay's Eastern Task Force landing the British forces and Vice Admiral Henry Hewitt's Western Task Force landing the US Army forces. The Royal Navy provided the principal covering forces for the amphibious landings, with Force H based out of Egypt and assigned to cover the eastern flank and provide feints towards the Greek coast for deception purposes, while Force Z from Gibraltar remained in the western Mediterranean to deal with any threats from the Italian fleet. A total of 2,590 ships took part in the operation, of which the Royal Navy was the predominant force with some 1,614 vessels, while the US Navy provided 945. The Royal Navy contributed most of the larger warships, including six battleships, two aircraft carriers, 15 cruisers, three monitors, and 106 destroyers, frigates, and corvettes. The US Navy deployed five cruisers and 48 destroyers. Landing ships and craft constituted much of the force, with 1,042 crewed by the Royal Navy and 700 from the US Navy.

The landing plan was complex since the various components were coming from ports across the Mediterranean, from Algeria to Egypt as well as Britain (Canadian 1st Division) and the United States (45th Division). The amphibious landing plans incorporated a large number of technical innovations, especially in regard to landing ships and landing craft. The American-built LST (landing ship tank) had been inspired by British concepts and was a major step forward in assault landings, since it was the first amphibious assault ship with true shore-to-shore capability. Sicily posed some challenges to its use, especially the presence of sandbars and runnels that threatened to limit its ability to land vehicles dry on the shore's edge. The US Navy's solution to this problem was another innovation, a type of pontoon that could be carried on the side of the LST and then deposited in the water to create a causeway over shallow water. The smaller LCT (landing craft tank) had been used in previous landings such as Dieppe, but would see a far more extensive use during *Husky*. One of the most critical innovations was the DUKW, an amphibious version of the US Army's 2½-ton truck, which proved exceptionally useful along Sicily's shallow southern beaches.

OPPOSING PLANS

AXIS PLANS

There was no consensus in Berlin and Rome over where the Allies would strike next. Hitler's strategic perception was that the Balkans were the most critical to Germany's military survival, owing to the importance of Romanian oil and the supply of critical raw materials from elsewhere in the region. The Italian and German high commands variously pointed to Sardinia, Sicily, Crete, and Greece as the next Allied objective. This led to a crippling dispersion of the already weakened Axis forces. To amplify this uncertainty, Britain conducted a deception campaign, with Operation *Mincemeat* as its most brilliant ploy. The body of a dead man was dressed in a British officer's uniform. A briefcase chained to the corpse contained phony documents addressed to General Sir Harold Alexander describing a forthcoming "Operation *Husky*" against Greece by General Sir Henry Maitland Wilson's forces in Egypt, an "Operation *Brimstone*" by Alexander's forces against Sardinia, and a deception campaign to convince the Germans that Sicily was the objective. The body was deposited off the Spanish coast by submarine on the night of April 30, 1943, on the presumption that it would wash ashore and be turned over to German officials. This indeed proved to be the case, and copies of the contents of the briefcase arrived in Berlin. Hitler was already inclined to view the Balkans as the main Allied objective and the *Mincemeat* documents bolstered his preconceptions. Between March 1943 and July 1943, Wehrmacht strength in the Balkans rose from eight to 18 divisions and those in Greece from one to eight; Sicily received barely two

Italian coastal defense doctrine focused on the protection of major ports. The Syracuse-Augusta stronghold was heavily fortified, including the Batteria Opera A on Cape Santa Panagia, which covered both ports. This turreted mount was built during World War I on the pattern of the famous Amalfi battery and was armed with twin Vickers 15in. guns, known in Italian navy service as the 381/40. This battery fired on British warships attempting to land special forces on June 10, but the guns were spiked and the crews retreated on the morning of July 11 before being captured by advancing British forces. (MHI)

Palermo had extensive coastal fortifications, which offered little defensive value when the US Army approached from landward. This is an Ansaldo 152/45 S.1911, a World War I siege gun built under license from the French Schneider company. It was deployed in the Palermo area for coast defense with two batteries of the army's 41º Gruppo d'artiglieria pesante. (NARA)

divisions. This was not solely attributable to the *Mincemeat* deception, but rather that Hitler's previous inclinations had been supported by *Mincemeat*.

Berlin's assessment of the situation was not shared by Rome. The Comando Supremo thought that Sardinia was the most likely target for the upcoming Allied operation, owing to its obvious potential as a forward base for the Allies to leapfrog into northern Italy and southern France. Both German and Italian theater commanders were far more concerned about the threat to Sicily. Kesselring and Guzzoni both felt that Sicily was a highly likely objective. The reinforcement of Sicily with two German divisions was a local initiative. The creation of the Division Sizilien was initiated by Baade, and the transfer of the Panzer-Division "Hermann Göring" was initiated by Kesselring with the acquiescence of Berlin. The location of the two divisions was the source of some controversy. Guzzoni wished to have both divisions located in southeastern Sicily owing to his assessment that this was the most likely locale for Allied landings. Kesselring was concerned that the Allies would want one of the western ports such as Palermo or Trapani, and so he ordered 15. Panzergrenadier-Division deployed there.

The real Axis strategic dilemma in the Mediterranean in the summer of 1943 was Italy's ultimate intention towards the Rome–Berlin alliance and its willingness to continue the war. The German foreign ministry was paying close attention to rumors of King Victor Emmanuel's disaffection with Mussolini and there was ample evidence of a crisis in the Italian government. By the spring of 1943, a toxic cynicism permeated Italian–German relations. In mid-May 1943, the German general staff completed contingency plans codenamed *Alarich* and *Konstantin* on Hitler's instructions. Operation *Alarich*, named appropriately enough after the sack of Rome by Goth invaders in ad 410, was entrusted to Erwin Rommel. The plan was to infiltrate four German divisions into Italy, followed by a dozen more divisions, to take over control of Italy. Operation *Konstantin* was a related scheme to disarm Italian forces in the Balkans in the event that Italy switched sides.

The threat posed by Allied airborne operations prompted the Italian army to form special anti-paratrooper units (NAP: Nuclei antiparacadutisti), usually relying on truck-mounted infantry. This is an Autocarro unificato Fiat 626 fitted with a Bredo 20mm mod. 35 in the rear-bed. (MHI)

On June 21, 1943, the Italians presented the Germans with a long list of weapons they needed to continue the war. At the same time, the Italian army was adamant that a strict limit be placed on the number of German divisions allowed into Italy for fear they would be used to impose a new government subservient to Germany. Berlin regarded the extravagant weapons demand, and the likely German refusal, as an Italian pretext for giving up on the war. The mistrust on both sides was entirely justified; the Italian government was plotting ways to extract itself from the war and the Germans were plotting to take control of Italy.

ALLIED PLANS

In the wake of the Casablanca conference, the Allies created the Force 141 headquarters in the suburbs of Algiers to formulate the Operation *Husky* plan. Its first "Tactical Appreciation" was released on March 15, but received little attention from senior Allied tactical commanders, who were focused on the conclusion of the Tunisian campaign. The two predominant tactical considerations in the plans were airfields and ports. Tedder and the other air chiefs insisted that the operation needed to seize airfields as soon as possible. The bases on Malta were already beyond their capacity and Sicily was on the outer edge of the range of many of the fighters such as Spitfires. Sicilian airbases would immeasurably aid in achieving air dominance over the island. The navy chiefs wanted the planners to focus on the need for port facilities to supply the army units once the landings had taken place. The best port on Sicily was Messina, with a daily capacity of 4,000–5,000 tons, but this objective was ruled out immediately since it was so heavily fortified and beyond the range of fighters based on Malta. The next best port on Sicily was Palermo on the north coast, while Catania and Syracuse on the east coast could each handle more than 1,000 tons of cargo per day.

The original plans for Operation *Husky* attempted to meld the airbase and port requirements into a complicated scheme of sequential landings. The British Eastern Task Force would conduct four separate landings on D-Day to capture airfields and smaller ports, followed by a main landing on D+3 against Catania. The American Western Task Force would begin its landings on D+2 to capture the airfields at Sciacca and Castelvetrano, followed by D+5 landings on either side of Palermo to capture the port. This scheme immediately ran into opposition since it was overly complex and would lead to a dispersion of Allied forces. Eisenhower suggested a concentration of landings in the southeast, but at first this was rejected owing to the need for the port of Palermo in the northwest. By the end of March 1943, Montgomery became involved in the planning, and he was very critical of the weakness of the British landings in the southeast. One option would be to use one of the American divisions from the Western Task Force to seize Gela on the western side of the British beachheads.

By late April, the naval commanders were becoming increasingly worried about the threat of Axis airpower against the invasion fleet after reading the alarming intelligence assessments, and so more supportive of Tedder's push for capturing airfields. British corps commander Lt. Gen. Oliver Leese suggested abandoning the multi-pronged concept in favor of a unified attack against the southeast corner of Sicily. With its cluster of airbases and proximity to the ports of Syracuse, Augusta, and Catania, this area became more and more attractive as the central focus of Allied operations. Nevertheless, the conference again deadlocked, forcing Eisenhower to convene yet another conference on May 2. This time, Montgomery personally made a strong case for the unified approach, which was supported by both Eisenhower and Alexander, ending the debate. Neither Patton nor Bradley was entirely happy with the plan since the Seventh US Army no longer had a major objective beyond acting as a flank guard for the British 8th Army. On the other hand, neither was inclined to make a strenuous protest, recognizing that, in Bradley's words, the whole planning process had taken place "in a fog of indecision, confusion, and conflicting plans." Now at least, a degree of unanimity had finally prevailed.

The May 19 *Husky* plan was primarily focused on the initial landings and the rapid seizure of airfields near the landing area. The next phase of the land campaign was concentrated in the British sector, with an aim to capture the ports of Augusta and Catania, as well as the airfield complex around Gerbini. The final phase of the campaign, "the reduction of the island" was not tightly defined in terms of objectives or focus and this would be the root of later difficulties.

One of the most useful technical innovations that saw its debut during Operation *Husky* was the DUKW amphibious 2½-ton truck. This not only provided the capability to move supplies ashore like conventional landing craft, but also, on reaching the shoreline, the DUKW could continue to its destination beyond the beachhead, greatly simplifying logistics, and helping to reduce the usual congestion in the beachhead. This DUKW is moving through Port Empedocle on July 25, 1943. (NARA)

THE CAMPAIGN

On July 9, the Allied convoys began heading out from the North African coast for rendezvous off Malta. A strong summer storm struck the fleet, but Allied meteorologists predicted that it would moderate in the pre-dawn hours of D-Day, July 10. An Italian reconnaissance aircraft spotted Allied convoys off Pantelleria in the pre-dawn hours of July 9, followed by sporadic sightings the rest of the day. The German garrison on Sicily was put on alert on July 9 at 1840hrs; Gen. Guzzoni issued a preliminary alert at 1900hrs and a state of emergency at 0100hrs to the Italian garrison, including instructions to begin demolitions along the southern coast. Allied aircraft conducted a series of heavy air raids on the evening of July 9 in preparation for the attack. Although the Allied naval commanders had urged a thorough pre-landing naval bombardment, the army commanders had opted for a landing in the pre-dawn darkness with the bombardments used largely for diversionary purposes. Warships stood by to deal with any Italian coastal artillery batteries.

AIRBORNE ASSAULT: *HUSKY 1*

Operation *Husky* included the first large-scale use of airborne troops to support an Allied amphibious assault. Allied airborne operations were still in their infancy, and the *Husky* night landings greatly increased the risk. The most significant problem was the lack of adequate navigation aids for the transport pilots, who were forced to rely on visual identification at night for the airdrops.

The US mission was codenamed *Husky 1* and was conducted by Col. James Gavin's Combat Team 505, consisting of 505th Parachute Infantry Regiment (PIR) reinforced by 3/504th PIR and totaling 3,405 paratroopers. Its mission was to seize key road junctions and bridges to shield the 1st Infantry Division landings near Gela. *Husky 1* was preceded by US bomber strikes against Sicilian airfields in the landing area, the drop of dummy paratroopers at scattered locations, and the use of radar-jamming B-17 bombers to blind Axis radars. The 226 C-47 transports were obliged to take a convoluted route to the drop zone to avoid flying over the Allied fleets for fear of provoking friendly-fire incidents. The stream of transports flew at a height of 500ft over the sea to avoid radar detection. Aside from the difficulties of low-altitude navigation, the remnants of a summer storm disrupted the approach. The airdrops began around midnight on July 9–10.

Operation *Husky*, July 10, 1943

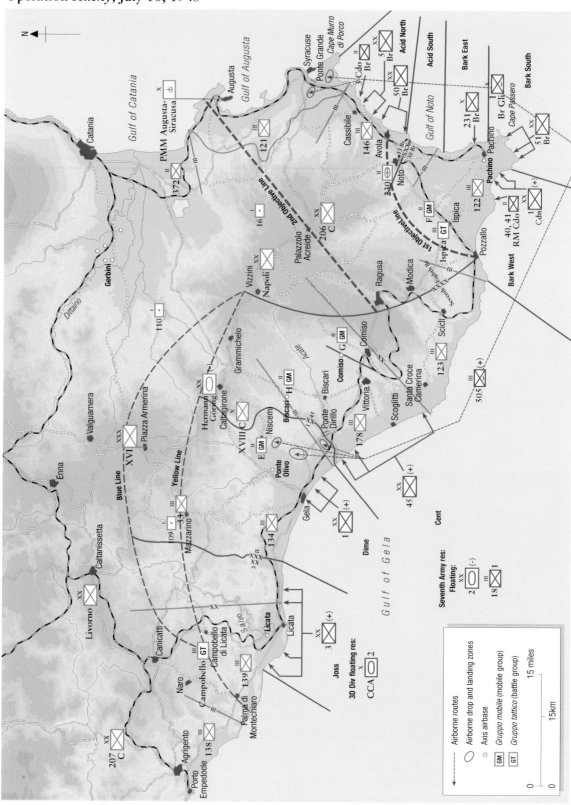

N

Legend:
- Airborne routes
- Airborne drop and landing zones
- Axis airbase
- GM *Gruppo mobile* (mobile group)
- GT *Gruppo tattico* (battle group)

0 — 15 miles
0 — 15km

Although the troop carrier squadrons thought that they had dropped about 80 percent of the paratroopers on or near the proper drop zones, in fact only about 15 percent of the paratroopers had landed anywhere near their intended drop zones.

The leading battalion, 3/504th PIR, landed near its objective but was badly dispersed. Some groups coalesced near Castel Nocera and were able to beat back Italian counterattacks. The 3/505th PIR's main objective, the Niscemi road junction, was captured by Co. I, but most of Co. G landed 3 miles away near the Acate River and the remainder of the battalion was scattered 10–15 miles from the drop zone near Vittoria. Much of the 1/505th PIR landed in the British sector nearly 50 miles east of the Niscemi road objective. Company A landed about two miles from the Niscemi objective and attacked Italian pillboxes along the Niscemi road. The 45th Division was the unintended beneficiary of the airborne drops after much of 2/505th PIR unintentionally landed in front of its beachhead. The final troop carrier group carrying the regimental headquarters and specialist troops had the most severe navigation problems and scattered its hapless paratroopers from Syracuse across southeastern Sicily.

Overall, *Husky 1* was officially judged a "qualified success," in spite of the abysmal inaccuracy of the airdrops. The paratroopers were able to secure many of the objectives owing to the weak resistance of the Italian coastal units. Furthermore, units that landed away from their targets used their own initiative and began attacking targets of opportunity all along the Sicilian coast. These sporadic and scattered outbursts of fighting convinced the Italians that they were facing a much larger and more powerful force, and this contributed to the confused Axis reaction to the landings in the American sector on the morning of July 10.

AIRBORNE ASSAULT: *LADBROKE*

The *Ladbroke* mission was far more controversial than the American landings, depending on glider forces instead of paratroopers. Since there were not enough British Horsa gliders available in the theater, the assault used American Waco CG-4A Hadrian gliders. The British pilots were not familiar with the type, the gliders arrived too late to conduct sufficient training, and the American C-47 wing assigned to tow the gliders did not have much glider-towing experience. As if this was not bad enough, the commander of the British glider pilots objected to the use of gliders in a night landing, owing to the lack of any type of navigation aid and the difficulties of the landing zones. These criticisms were rashly dismissed by the brigade leadership. In contrast to the American mission, which had a loose objective of securing the area behind the beachhead, *Ladbroke* was specifically aimed at seizing the Ponte Grande bridge and four other objectives.

A total of 109 C-47s and 27 Albemarles towed the 136 Hadrians, while Halifaxes and Albemarles towed the eight larger Horsa gliders. Owing to mishaps at the airbases in Tunisia, only 137 gliders of the original 144 took part in the mission. About 109 to 119 aircraft reached satisfactory launch points off Syracuse and, in the face of strong headwinds from the June 9 gale, the transport pilots increased their release altitudes by about 300ft. The returning transport pilots thought that 95 percent of the gliders had reached the landing zones; in fact the nighttime releases over the sea in the face of headwinds led to disaster. Not only did the transport pilots have a hard time judging the distance to shore, but the glider pilots as well found it difficult to orient themselves in the dark. A total of 76 Hadrians and three Horsas landed at sea. Only 49 Hadrians and five Horsas reached dry land and, of these, only about a dozen were close to their objective. Casualties in the initial landing totaled 605, of whom 326 were presumed drowned.

Horsa glider 133 with No. 15 Platoon of 2nd South Staffordshires, under Lt. Lennard Withers, was the only glider to land near the Ponte Grande bridge intact. The platoon split in two, assaulted an Italian pillbox, and captured the bridge without casualties. Sappers removed demolition charges and wiring and the platoon set up a defense position. As dawn approached, troops from gliders that had landed nearby gradually made their way to the bridge, totaling seven officers and 80 men by dawn. The glider attack managed to seize the most important objective, but was unable to secure any of the other four targets.

The Waco CG-4A Hadrian glider carrying part of No. 14 Platoon of B Company, the South Staffordshires, hit a power line before crash-landing in a tomato field during Operation *Ladbroke*. The rest of the platoon in another glider crashed at sea. (NARA)

8TH ARMY LANDINGS

The left flank of the Allied landings was the British 13th Corps, codenamed Acid, with the 5th Division landing at Acid North and the 50th Division at Acid South. The sector was bounded by the heavily defended PMM Siracusa-Augusta naval base on its right, while the center of the beaches was held by Col. Cancellera's 146° Reggimento costieri of the 206° Divisione costiera. The coastal defense forces were alerted early on the morning of July 10 and NAP anti-paratroop truck patrols were active in the sector, where they reported capturing 174 British and American airborne troops.

The British landings were spearheaded by special forces: the SAS Special Raiding Squadron overwhelmed the Italian 152mm gun Batteria Lamba Dori on Cape Murro di Porco at the northern edge of Acid North; the No. 3 Commando eliminated the coastal battery near Cassibile. The Acid North beaches were within the defensive zone of the PMM Siracusa-Augusta and so the area received harassing fire from Italian coastal batteries farther to the north. The landings by the 5th Division were complicated by the rough water, but 17th Brigade was ashore by 0500hrs and moving to secure the towns along the coast, while 15th Brigade landed late and on the wrong beaches. Aside from shelling from the naval base, Italian resistance on the landing beaches was weak. The 50th Division landing around Avola had a difficult time in the water owing to the remnants of the summer gale, and 151st Brigade was not fully ashore until after 0600hrs but faced little opposition.

Troops of the Seaforth Highlanders of 51st Highland Division come ashore at Bark South beach on July 10 from LCI(L)-249. (NARA)

LCT-420 of 3rd LST(2) Flotilla lands a M3A1 scout car at Bark South Beach on the morning of July 10, 1943, using an improvised raft pontoon ramp. (NARA)

The 30th Corps landings took place on the "Bark" beaches on either side of the Pachino peninsula. This area was defended by Col. D'Apollonio's 122° Reggimento costieri of the 206° Divisione costiera. The 231st Malta Brigade went ashore on Bark East at the junction between 13th and 30th Corps. The 51st Division landed on Bark South on either side of Portopalo Bay against negligible resistance. The Canadian 1st Division debarked on Bark West on the western side of the peninsula with modest delays. The assault on the Bark beaches was capped off by landings of 40 and 41 Royal Marine Commando to secure the extreme left flank of the 8th Army landing area. As in the case of the neighboring 13th Corps landing zone, Italian resistance was mostly confined to sporadic encounters with troops in pillboxes; active coastal batteries were suppressed with naval gunfire.

The Italian navy stronghold at Syracuse was abandoned on July 10 after most of its coastal batteries had been destroyed by their crews. Italian navy strongholds used artillery trains for mobile coastal defense, and this is the TA 102/1/T that was stationed on the rail line north of Syracuse between Cape Santo Panagia and the Magnisi peninsula. It was armed with four 102/35mm pedestal-mounted dual-purpose guns and is seen here being inspected by British troops. (NARA)

SEVENTH US ARMY LANDINGS

The American landings faced significantly more resistance than the British beaches, but not enough seriously to impede the assault. The operations proved somewhat more difficult to carry out, as the southern beaches were more exposed to the remnants of the July 9 gale and the water was rough.

The right flank of the American landings was the Cent Force from 45th Division at Scoglitti. This beach was in the sector of Col. Sebastianello's 178° Reggimento, XVIII Brigata costiere. As mentioned earlier, US paratroop drops had landed inadvertently in this sector, and the Italian infantry battalions were already engaged with the paratroopers when the amphibious landings occurred. This division had shipped out directly from the United States and suffered from a combination of inexperienced boat crews and heavy surf at the two main landing beaches. Three Italian gun batteries fired on the landing site but were suppressed by naval gunfire. In spite of the confusion and commotion on the beach in the early morning hours, 45th Division was moving off the beaches by afternoon and against little Italian resistance.

The only beach to see much resistance at all was 1st Division's Dime Force, landing near the port of Gela. Although Gela was a fairly minor port, it had enough of a dock area that it had received far more lavish defenses than most of the other beaches assaulted on D-Day. It was defended by Maj. Rubellino's 429° Battaglione, 134° Reggimento costiere. The city's main pier was prepared for demolition and destroyed in the pre-dawn hours before the arrival of US troops. This sector was the primary landing area of the *Husky 1* paratroop drop; the Italian garrison was heavily engaged with the paratroopers prior to the landing and already had suffered about 45 percent casualties during the confused nighttime fighting.

The Royal Navy monitor HMS *Abercrombie* provides fire support off Gela during the pre-dawn landings on June 10. (NARA)

The 1st Division landing force was reinforced on the left flank with Col. William Darby's Force X consisting of the 1st and 4th Rangers supported by combat engineers. The searchlights of Italian coastal batteries illuminated the landing force before finally being hit by gunfire from the destroyer USS *Shubrick* around 0310hrs. Force X landed on either side of the demolished pier but found the beach to be heavily mined and under continual machine-gun fire from a multitude of pillboxes. The Italian defenses were overcome in the pre-dawn hours and the town secured by early morning. In contrast to the town defenses, the two regiments of 1st Division landing east of Gela encountered very little Italian resistance.

On the far left of the US landing zone was 3rd Division's Joss Force, landing on either side of Licata. This sector was defended by 384° Battaglione of Col. Altini's 134° Reggimento costiere, reinforced with coastal artillery including two batteries of 105/27 guns of the CXLV Gruppo artigliere, the 75/34 guns of the 81° Batteria battery, and the navy's 76-II-T coastal artillery train armed with four dual-purpose 76/40 guns. In contrast to the other beaches, the Italian artillery fire was so persistent that, on a number of occasions, landing waves had to be held off until the navy could deal with the threat. Fire from the mobile artillery train shut Beach Red around dawn until silenced by the destroyer USS *Buck*, and renewed fire from batteries on Monte Sole was finally silenced around 0715hrs by the cruiser USS *Brooklyn*. The coastal batteries around Licata put up a much more spirited defense than on the other beaches and the batteries on Monte Desusino behind Blue Beach were also attacked by the US warships. In contrast to the artillery troops, the Italian infantry showed little will to resist. The 538° Battaglione was ordered to counterattack, but was quickly stopped. The 3rd Division captured nearly 3,000 prisoners on the first day during its rapid drive inland.

Elements from II Corps come ashore at Gela from an LST, including towed 90mm guns of 401st AAA Battalion (Mobile). The Italian prisoners in the foreground suggest that this photo was taken after the fighting in Gela on July 11. (NARA)

THE INITIAL AXIS RESPONSE: AMERICAN SECTOR

The strongest Axis response to the Allied landings took place against Gela with the Italian forces in the lead. Local resources, including Gruppo Mobile E, were ordered to attack immediately and Guzzoni instructed both the Divisione Livorno and the two battlegroups of the Panzer-Division "Hermann Göring" near Caltagirone to stage a counterattack.

After dawn, 4/501° Battaglione costiere, supported by a platoon of R-35 tanks, bumped into the defenses set up by Col. Gorham's 1/505th PIR near Priolo and were dispersed by small-arms fire and naval gunfire. At the same time, the bulk of Ten. Col. Davide Conte's Gruppo Mobile E moved down Highway 117 toward Gela farther to the west. This force was hit repeatedly by naval gunfire that stripped away much of its infantry, but the R-35 tank company and an accompanying towed anti-gun company continued into Gela.

In the meantime, the Divisione Livorno had dispatched its nearest unit, 3/33° Regt. fant. from Butera towards Gela, approaching the western outskirts of Gela. The western part of town was held by Darby's Ranger force, who had positioned some captured Italian field guns at the outskirts of the town. The inexperienced Italian infantry bunched up in the fields outside Gela, making them very vulnerable to the artillery and machine-gun fire, and their attack was broken up before reaching the town. While the fighting was going on to the west, the Italian tank column pushed its way into town from the north. The Rangers began a cat-and-mouse hunt against the tanks using bazookas and improvised explosive charges, forcing the survivors to retreat.

The German attack on Gela took more time to build up steam. Generalleutnant Conrath planned to attack the Gela beachhead with a two-pronged attack: a battlegroup from the east, consisting of the two truck-mounted infantry battalions of Panzergrenadier-Regiment "Hermann Göring"

Naval gunfire played a critical role in breaking up the attack by Divisione Livorno against the western side of Gela on July 11. This is a view from the bridge of LST-325 heading into Gela with portions of Kool Force. The cruiser USS *Boise* can be seen over the bow, engaging targets ashore. (NARA)

TANK ATTACK AT GELA, JULY 10, 1943 (pp. 42–43)

The most active Italian tank unit in the opening phase of the Sicily campaign was the 101° Battaglione carri, which was equipped with about 50 war-booty French Renault R-35 infantry tanks. This battalion had been created in Siena on July 27, 1941, as part of the 131° Rgt. carro of the Centauro armored division in Friuli. The battalion was broken off in January 1942 and dispatched to Sicily along with 102° Battaglione. The battalion did not fight as a unit, but its companies were broken up to form the nucleus of the four *Gruppi Mobili* assigned to XVI Corpo in eastern Sicily: Gruppi Mobili D, E, F, and G. Each separate company typically had 16 tanks.

The scene here shows the attack by Gruppo Mobili E against Gela on July 10, 1943. This mobile group consisted of Capitano Giuseppe Granieri's 1ª Compagnia of this tank battalion along with a 47mm antitank gun company, an infantry company from 501° Battaglione costiero, a motorcycle company, a battery of 75/18 howitzers, and a 20mm antiaircraft cannon section. Around 0530hrs on July 10, a tank platoon was assigned to support 429° Battaglione costiero, which was involved in a fight with paratroopers of Gorham's 1/505th PIR around Priolo but the attack was broken up by naval gunfire. The mobile group attacked

Gela itself later in the morning down Highway 117, but much of the supporting infantry and other troops were stripped away from the tanks by naval gunfire. A portion of the company's tanks and the antitank gun company fought their way into the town where they encountered Col. Darby's "Force X," consisting of 1st and 4th Rangers along with 1/39th Combat Engineers. The engineers were equipped with bazookas and began to hunt the tanks through the narrow town streets. The Rangers had few antitank weapons, but made up improvised satchel charges using explosives, which they hurled on the tanks from second-story windows. Colonel Darby himself **(1)** raced back to the beach in his jeep, found a 37mm antitank gun **(2)**, and brought it back to the town where he knocked out at least one tank **(3)**. After suffering heavy losses, the spearhead of Gruppo Mobili E retreated from Gela. The remnants of the unit fought again on July 11 supporting III/34° Rgt. fant. of the Livorna division along Highway 117 against 3/26th Infantry.

The 2ª Compagnia, 131° Battaglioni carro took part in the Gruppo Mobili F attack on the British and Canadian forces near Pachino on July 10, while 3ª Compagnia took part in the Gruppo Mobili D battle around Solarino and Floridia on July 11.

Armored elements of Kool Force, part of Combat Command B, 2nd Armored Division, went ashore on July 10–11 at Gela. These two M2 half-tracks are part of the headquarters company of 67th Armored Regiment. (NARA)

supported by the Tiger tank company, and from the west, consisting of Oberst Urban's Panzer-Regiment "Hermann Göring" supported by the divisional reconnaissance and engineer battalions. The advance was a complete fiasco owing to the inexperience of the unit, poor leadership, and repeated disruptions caused by small skirmishes with groups of American paratroopers. The tank column finally managed to get moving and bumped into defensive positions of 2/16th Infantry and 1/505th Parachute Infantry near Priolo. The Panzers lacked an accompanying infantry force aside from divisional reconnaissance and engineer troops, and two separate attacks were beat back with small arms fire and naval gunfire. The eastern Panzergrenadier group collided with 1/180th Infantry and initially backed off when hit by field artillery support. The accompanying Tiger tanks fumbled around, in part owing to mechanical problems. A second assault later in the afternoon led by Conrath himself overwhelmed the 1/180th Infantry defenses but was stopped when 3/180th Infantry arrived on the scene. The performance of the tank column on July 10 was so embarrassing that its commander was relieved that day by Gen.Lt. von Senger und Etterlin; the Panzergrenadier commander was sacked the next day.

The blown-up wreckage of a PzKpfw IV tank of Panzer-Regiment "Hermann Göring" in the fields north of Gela after the failed July 11 counterattack against the US 1st Division. (NARA)

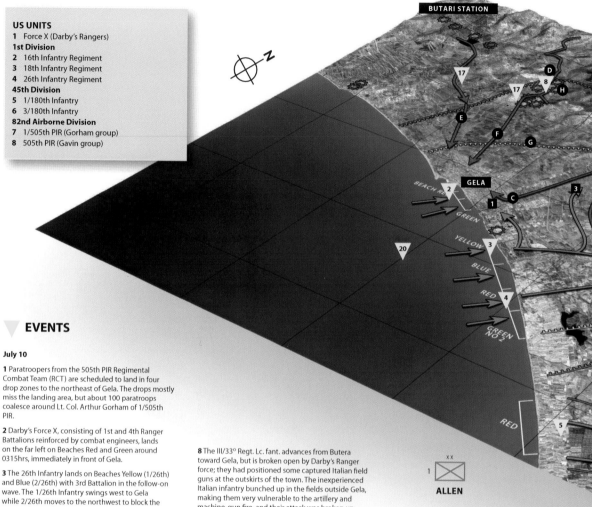

Note: Gridlines are shown at intervals of 5 km/3.125 miles

US UNITS
1 Force X (Darby's Rangers)
1st Division
2 16th Infantry Regiment
3 18th Infantry Regiment
4 26th Infantry Regiment
45th Division
5 1/180th Infantry
6 3/180th Infantry
82nd Airborne Division
7 1/505th PIR (Gorham group)
8 505th PIR (Gavin group)

BUTARI STATION

GELA

ALLEN

▼ EVENTS

July 10

1 Paratroopers from the 505th PIR Regimental Combat Team (RCT) are scheduled to land in four drop zones to the northeast of Gela. The drops mostly miss the landing area, but about 100 paratroops coalesce around Lt. Col. Arthur Gorham of 1/505th PIR.

2 Darby's Force X, consisting of 1st and 4th Ranger Battalions reinforced by combat engineers, lands on the far left on Beaches Red and Green around 0315hrs, immediately in front of Gela.

3 The 26th Infantry lands on Beaches Yellow (1/26th) and Blue (2/26th) with 3rd Battalion in the follow-on wave. The 1/26th Infantry swings west to Gela while 2/26th moves to the northwest to block the approaches to the town.

4 The 16th Infantry lands on Beaches Red 2 (2/16th) and Green 2 (1/16th) with 3rd Battalion in the follow-on wave. Troops head toward Piano Lupo to meet up with the paratroopers.

5 The neighboring 45th Division lands to the southeast, with 180th Infantry on Beach Red, nearest 1st Division. The 1/180th Infantry moves into the hills over the beach during the morning.

6 Gruppo Mobile E moves down Route 117 around dawn with the R-35 tanks in the lead. From 0806hrs to 0920hrs, the cruiser USS *Savannah* and destroyer *Shubrick* fire on the column. The naval fire strips the infantry support from the tanks and about seven continue into Gela, where they fight with Force X in the streets before being forced to withdraw later in the morning.

7 Around 0830hrs, a column from 4/501° Battaglione costiere supported by a few R-35 tanks bumps into Gorham's paratroopers at Casa de Priolo between Piano Lupo and Niscemi. The approaching 16th Infantry calls in naval fire and starting at 0842hrs, the destroyer USS *Jeffers* and the cruiser *Boise* fire on the Italian column. The tanks pass through the fire but eventually are halted on contact with 16th Infantry and return back up the road to Niscemi.

8 The III/33° Regt. Lc. fant. advances from Butera toward Gela, but is broken open by Darby's Ranger force; they had positioned some captured Italian field guns at the outskirts of the town. The inexperienced Italian infantry bunched up in the fields outside Gela, making them very vulnerable to the artillery and machine-gun fire, and their attack was broken up before reaching the town.

9 An attack by elements of Panzer-Regiment HG from Niscemi approaches 2/16th Infantry in the hills near Priolo but is halted by fire from the destroyer *Jeffers* around 1515hrs.

10 The accompanying attack from Biscari by the Panzergrenadier *Kampfgruppe* supported by Tiger tanks of 2./sc. Pz.Abt. 504 overruns elements of 1/180th Infantry along Highway 115 and captures the battalion commander. The arrival of 3/180th Infantry halts the German attack and the Germans withdraw in the late afternoon.

July 11

11 Around 0847hrs, the cruiser *Boise* and destroyer *Glennon* begin engaging Hermann Göring *Kampfgruppe* forming up in the vicinity of Niscemi.

12 The Panzer-Regiment HG advances in two columns, with II./Pz.Rgt. HG attacking out of the Ponte Olivo airbase down Highway 117 towards Gela against 26th Infantry and I./Pz.Rgt. HG attacking down the Niscemi-Priolo road towards the 16th Infantry defenses. The regiment loses six of its nine 57mm antitank guns in the fighting along with many of its 37mm antitank guns. The regiment reports "We are being overrun by tanks."

13 Starting around 0827hrs, the cruiser *Savannah* begins engaging the *Kampfgruppe* of II./Pz.Rgt. HG moving down Highway 117. The tank columns are able to push past elements of 16th and 26th Infantry and scattered paratroopers of 505th PIR, which lack sufficient antitank weapons.

14 Spearheads of the two Panzer columns attempt to link up around the Farello airfield. Beginning at 1040hrs, the cruiser *Boise* begins firing on the German spearheads that have reached this area. The 32nd Field Artillery Battalion, recently arrived on the beach on DUKWs, moves into the dunes and begins firing on the German tanks with 105mm howitzers, supported by 16th Cannon Company and four M4A1 medium tanks from Kool Force.

15 The destroyer USS *Butler* begins to fire on elements of II./Pz.Rgt. HG on Highway 117.

16 The Panzergrenadier *Kampfgruppe* from Biscari forces Co. F, 180th Infantry to withdraw from Ponte Dirillo, but the remainder of 2/180th Infantry hold their positions with the support of 171st Field Artillery Battalion located on the beach. This *Kampfgruppe* HG is fired on repeatedly during the day, starting with fire from the destroyer USS *Beatty* and continuing through the day with the assistance of three other destroyers, totaling 1,796 rounds.

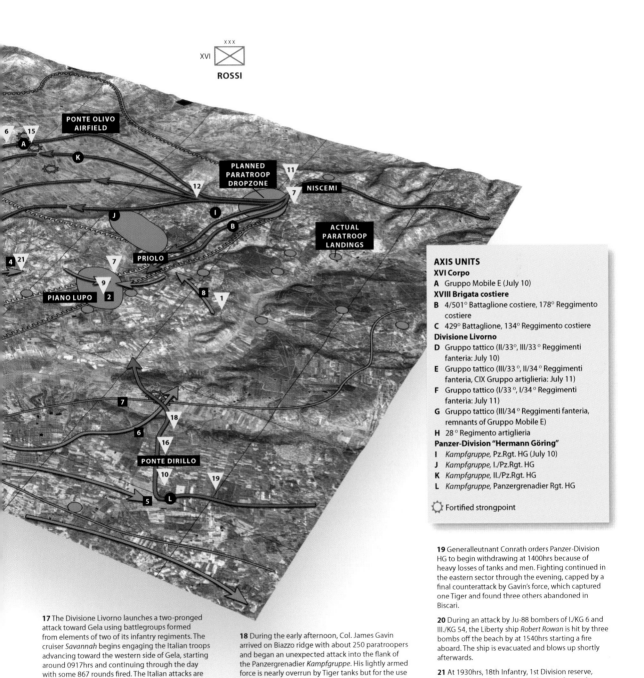

XVI ⊠ xxx

ROSSI

PONTE OLIVO AIRFIELD

6 15
A
K
12
PLANNED PARATROOP DROPZONE
11
7 NISCEMI
J
I
B
ACTUAL PARATROOP LANDINGS
4 21
7
PRIOLO
9
8 1
PIANO LUPO
2
7
18
6
16
PONTE DIRILLO
10 19
5 L

AXIS UNITS
XVI Corpo
A Gruppo Mobile E (July 10)
XVIII Brigata costiere
B 4/501° Battaglione costiere, 178° Reggimento costiere
C 429° Battaglione, 134° Reggimento costiere
Divisione Livorno
D Gruppo tattico (II/33°, III/33 ° Reggimenti fanteria: July 10)
E Gruppo tattico (III/33 °, II/34 ° Reggimenti fanteria, CIX Gruppo artiglieria: July 11)
F Gruppo tattico (I/33 °, I/34 ° Reggimenti fanteria: July 11)
G Gruppo tattico (III/34 ° Reggimenti fanteria, remnants of Gruppo Mobile E)
H 28 ° Regimento artiglieria
Panzer-Division "Hermann Göring"
I *Kampfgruppe*, Pz.Rgt. HG (July 10)
J *Kampfgruppe*, I./Pz.Rgt. HG
K *Kampfgruppe*, II./Pz.Rgt. HG
L *Kampfgruppe*, Panzergrenadier Rgt. HG

✿ Fortified strongpoint

17 The Divisione Livorno launches a two-pronged attack toward Gela using battlegroups formed from elements of two of its infantry regiments. The cruiser *Savannah* begins engaging the Italian troops advancing toward the western side of Gela, starting around 0917hrs and continuing through the day with some 867 rounds fired. The Italian attacks are eventually beaten off by the combination of naval gunfire as well as artillery fire and small arms from Force X inside Gela.

18 During the early afternoon, Col. James Gavin arrived on Biazzo ridge with about 250 paratroopers and began an unexpected attack into the flank of the Panzergrenadier *Kampfgruppe*. His lightly armed force is nearly overrun by Tiger tanks but for the use of 75mm pack howitzers at point-blank ranges and the arrival of two 57mm antitank guns from 179th Infantry.

19 Generalleutnant Conrath orders Panzer-Division HG to begin withdrawing at 1400hrs because of heavy losses of tanks and men. Fighting continued in the eastern sector through the evening, capped by a final counterattack by Gavin's force, which captured one Tiger and found three others abandoned in Biscari.

20 During an attack by Ju-88 bombers of I./KG 6 and III./KG 54, the Liberty ship *Robert Rowan* is hit by three bombs off the beach by at 1540hrs starting a fire aboard. The ship is evacuated and blows up shortly afterwards.

21 At 1930hrs, 18th Infantry, 1st Division reserve, begins to move forward to reinforce its forward elements for a counterattack toward Niscemi around midnight.

AXIS COUNTERATTACK ON GELA BEACHHEAD, JULY 10–11
The US 1st Division "Big Red One" beats off an armored counterattack by two Axis divisions during the first days of Sicily campaign

Although the Italian and German attacks were worrisome, the Seventh US Army units made good progress off the beaches on July 10. Patton decided to land parts of the Kool Force reserve from 2nd Armored Division, but most of the troops were from 41st Armored Infantry rather than the tank units because of problems landing tanks in the soft sand. Major-General Allen of 1st Infantry Division was anxious to get tanks ashore after the encounters with enemy tanks that afternoon, but the first ten medium tanks were not ashore until the pre-dawn hours of July 11.

On the night of July 10–11, Guzzoni ordered the Divisione Livorno and Panzer-Division "Hermann Göring" to coordinate their attacks the next day. Conrath and Chirielson met at the Italian corps headquarters in the pre-dawn hours and planned a joint attack starting at 0600hrs. The Panzer-Division "Hermann Göring" attack followed the same general direction as the previous day's attack. Divisione Livorno sent four infantry battalions down the roads leading into Gela from the west and alongside Highway 117.

The II./Pz.Rgt. HG tank attack crunched through the 26th Infantry toward Gela and was brought under fire by Darby's Rangers with their captured Italian artillery, as well as two battalions of 105mm howitzers of the divisional artillery. The Italian 3/34° Rgt. fant., advancing in parallel to the Panzers, was also hit by the artillery and stopped before reaching the town. In the center, I./Pz.Rgt. HG, under Conrath's direct command, pushed down to the west of the 16th Infantry positions heading for Gela across open ground. The 16th Infantry pulled back towards Piano Lupo. In the east, Pz.Gren.Rgt. HG forced 2/180th Infantry to retreat back towards the beaches, but an artillery battalion and naval gunfire support halted the German pursuit. By mid-morning, the two Panzer battalions of Pz.Rgt. HG had joined up on the outskirts of Gela, and Divisione Livorno sent another infantry battalion to reinforce the attack towards Gela. Guzzoni's headquarters reported that the 1st Division was re-embarking and fleeing

This is the Italian strongpoint at Ponte Dirillo, located on the hill overlooking the bridge over the Agate River, with the typical dome-shaped "Caposaldo" bunkers. The artillery revetment contained a war-booty French 75mm M1897 "Typ maroc." This strongpoint was at the northwest end of the Biazza ridge, where Col. James Gavin's group from the 3/505th Parachute Infantry Regiment fought against the attack by Panzergrenadier-Regiment "Hermann Göring" on July 11.

Gela, based on a mistaken radio intercept. The German tank attack, lacking sufficient infantry, had pushed through the US infantry positions without gaining firm control and American units on the beaches were rallying to repulse the German onslaught.

Although the situation looked bleak, the Rangers in Gela had established radio contact with warships offshore. The growing Italian infantry force on the western outskirts of Gela was pummeled by destroyer and cruiser fire, and withdrew after suffering crippling losses. In the center, 32nd Field Artillery Battalion, recently arrived on the beach on DUKWs, moved into the dunes and began firing directly at the German tanks with 105mm howitzers, supported by 16th Cannon Company and four M4A1 medium tanks. The infantry knocked out several more Panzers with antitank guns and bazookas. Panzer-Regiment "Hermann Göring" began withdrawing in the face of this fusillade.

In the eastern sector, Col. Gavin unexpectedly arrived on the flank of the Pz.Gren.Rgt. HG attack with an assortment of paratroopers he had collected over the previous day, and this force began advancing from the Biazzo ridge. The pugnacious paratroopers were ill equipped to deal with the accompanying Tiger tanks and forced to use 75mm pack howitzers at point-blank ranges. Eventually, two 57mm antitank guns arrived from the 179th Infantry and, once forward observers arrived, heavy artillery finally pummeled the eastern battlegroup and the Tigers began to withdraw.

At midday, senior Axis commanders believed that they had secured a victory in the Gela sector. Guzzoni instructed Conrath that, once he secured Gela, he should withdraw his forces back inland to Caltagirone with an aim to move them back eventually to Catania Plain to resist the British advance toward Messina. Senger und Etterlin arrived on the scene later and instructed Conrath to move east along the coast, cutting off elements of the 45th Division that were already well inland. By late afternoon, it was clear to Conrath that the attack had in fact failed. Ten of the 17 Tigers were lost,

Paratroopers of the 82nd Airborne Division inspect an abandoned Ford V3000S truck from Panzergrenadier-Regiment "Hermann Göring" lost during the July 11 counterattack. The division had only a single battalion of armored half-tracks, serving with Kampfgruppe Schmalz in the Catania sector, so the other battalions had to rely on ordinary trucks. (NARA)

along with about two-dozen PzKpfw III and PzKpfw IV tanks; the division had only 54 tanks serviceable out of the original 99 at the end of the day. German casualties were 630 dead and wounded. Divisione Livorno was even harder hit, suffering over 2,100 casualties. After tallying his unit's losses and facing persistent counterattacks, Conrath decided to pull back inland to avoid the constant naval shelling. The combined Italian–German attack on Gela on July 11 was by far the strongest Axis counteroffensive of the campaign. Although it delayed the advance in the center portion of the American landing zone, it had no long-term consequence.

Italian units also struck the 3rd Division around Licata using the Gruppo tattico Venturi, a battlegroup from 206° Divisione costiere reinforced with Semovente 90/53 tank destroyers from 161° and 163° Gruppi autocannoni. Although it slowed the 3rd Division advance, it failed to stop it. In the meantime, the battlegroups of 15. Panzergrenadier-Division in western Sicily had been ordered to move back toward eastern Sicily. Some elements of this division arrived in the hills over Licata and took part in the delaying actions on July 11.

The fighting in the American sector on July 11 ended in tragedy with yet another misbegotten airborne operation. There had been plans to reinforce 505th PIR by additional airborne drops after D-Day. It was widely recognized that one of the main threats would be potential fratricide if the transport force flew near the ships of the Western Task Force. The *Husky 2* operation was first scheduled for the night of July 10, but then rescheduled for the night of July 11–12. The ships of the Western Task Force had endured 23 air attacks on July 11, including a recent night attack; the army anti-aircraft gunners were trigger-happy as a result. The first element of the mission to the Farello airfield outside Gela flew the prescribed route but came under anti-aircraft fire from US forces both ashore and at sea. The follow-on waves endured even more anti-aircraft fire. Of the 144 C-47 transports on the mission, 23 were shot down and 37 suffered serious damage; the surviving pilots grimly joked that they would have been safer flying over enemy territory. Many of the paratroopers were dropped prematurely into the lines of 45th Division and numerous paratroopers were mistakenly wounded during the drop when mistaken for German paratroopers. The 504th Combat Team suffered 81 dead, 132 wounded, and 16 missing in the operation. After the fiasco, plans to conduct a glider reinforcement the next day were canceled.

THE INITIAL AXIS RESPONSE: BRITISH SECTOR

Ammiraglio Priamo Leonardi activated the PMM Augusta-Siracusa defenses in the pre-dawn hours. The southern perimeter of the naval base had already been penetrated by the glider assault on the Ponte Grande bridge and the SAS raid on Batteria Lamba Dori, and initial reports indicated that the Allies were landing in force on the Gulf of Noto south of the base. Guzzoni agreed to put units of the neighboring XVI Corpo at Leonardi's disposal.

An improvised battlegroup, the Gruppo Tattico Canicattini Bagni was formed before dawn from Maj. Guzzardi's 1/75° Rgt. fant. of Divisione Napoli supported by a battery of towed 75/27 howitzers. It set off around 0730hrs led by 95 bicycle troops, followed by 550 infantry in 22 trucks and

The only significant Italian tank forces on Sicily were two battalions of war-booty French Renault R-35 tanks. This is one of the tanks from Capitano Andrea Daconto's 2ª compagnia, 101º Battaglione carri with its distinctive ram's head insignia that took part in the attacks by Gruppo Mobili F against British and Canadian forces in the Pachino area on July 10–11. (NARA)

an additional 200 riflemen on foot. While this was under way, more distant units were ordered to begin moving toward Syracuse. The commander of Divisione Napoli, Gen. Fiumara, sent reinforcements to the other two battalions of 75º Rgt. under Col. Ronco, which departed from their base at Palazzalo. Gruppo Mobile D was ordered to move through Lentini and join Ronco's battlegroup on the western outskirts of Syracuse. The only significant German force in this sector was Kampfgruppe Schmalz from Panzer-Division "Hermann Göring" consisting of a half-track infantry battalion, an improvised infantry regiment with about two battalions of infantry, a company of StuG III assault guns, and supporting artillery and reconnaissance troops. Schmalz was ordered to attack via Augusta toward Syracuse to help defend the port.

A British section from 5th Division races along a stone wall during the fighting in the outskirts of the port of Augusta with Kampfgruppe Schmalz on July 11–12.

A patrol from the Princess Patricia's Canadian Light Infantry during the advance towards Modica on July 12 with the support of some commandeered Italian donkey carts. (NARA)

Guzzardi divided his battlegroup into three elements; one infantry company was sent to secure the Ponte Grande bridge while the other two companies were sent farther south to set up blocking positions between the bridge and the British landing beaches. During the early fighting, Guzzardi's troops collected about 160 British and American prisoners from units scattered over the area west of Syracuse. The attack against the British glider force at Ponte Grande began around 0800hrs and, after seven hours of fighting, more than 70 of the original 90 troops were casualties. Low on ammunition and surrounded on both sides, the battered British detachment was forced to surrender. While the fighting for Ponte Grande was taking place, a mechanized column from 2nd Battalion, Royal Scots Fusiliers of the advancing British 5th Division pushed through Guzzardi's southern infantry detachments and reached the bridge about a half-hour after the glider force had surrendered. What was left of the Italian battlegroup retreated towards Syracuse. The glider force's main contribution had been to prevent the demolition of the bridge.

A Sherman III of 50 RTR, 23rd Armoured Brigade on the streets of Francofonte on July 14 during the efforts to push north of Augusta. (NARA)

In spite of the failure of the *Ladbroke* mission to secure its numerous objectives, the British airborne landings had a profoundly disruptive effect on the Italian defenses in the Syracuse-Augusta stronghold. The scattered landings of gliders all around the Syracuse-Augusta area created the impression of a massive airborne attack. The Italians later accused the 400-man German Kriegsmarine garrison of triggering the debacle when they demolished their installation in Augusta harbor and retreated; the neighboring Italian detachments followed suit. Regardless of the German actions, the Italian defenses were crumbling on their own. The four coastal infantry battalions defending the ports retreated, often prior to contact with British forces. Coastal batteries had standing orders to demolish their guns rather than let them fall into enemy hands and, as the defending infantry units disappeared, the coastal batteries began spiking their guns. By 1700hrs, four hours before the British columns reached the city, a "psychosis of self-destruction spread like wildfire" through the Syracuse garrison according to the official Italian history. When British troops finally appeared on the heights overlooking Augusta Bay, Amm. Leonardi gave orders to the Augusta garrison to spike the fuel supplies and radio station. German troops from Kampfgruppe Schmalz appeared west of Augusta around 2000hrs on June 10, temporarily quieting the panic. Leonardi moved his command post to Melilli, alongside the lead German troops.

The 17th Brigade of the British 5th Division began moving into the outskirts of Syracuse, while the 13th Brigade pushed farther west toward Floridia to block the approaching Italian counterattack. The first clash between the British and German forces took place on the morning of July 11, when 17th Brigade ran into the forward positions of Kampfgruppe Schmalz on the southern approaches to Augusta. Although efforts were made to coordinate the defensive actions of this battlegroup with the Italian counterattack farther west, this did not occur and Schmalz attempted to conduct a delaying action in the hopes of establishing firmer defensive positions in front of Catania.

The attack by the Gruppo Tattico Ronco from Divisione Napoli on July 11 included the remnants of 1/75° Rgt., and Col. Ronco's own 2/75° Rgt. fant. This attack was coordinated with Gruppo Mobile D, which included

Among the early reinforcements in the Catania sector was a heavy weapons battalion of 1. Fallschirmjäger-Division, air-landed at Catania. This is a 7.5cm Leichtgeschütz LG 40 recoilless rifle, a rare weapon peculiar to the paratrooper force. (J. Janik)

18 Renault R-35 tanks, a company of infantry, and supporting artillery. The two forces met in Solarino before preparing to attack the 13th Brigade positions in Floridia. The attack began after dawn including a tank charge into Floridia, which suffered heavy losses at the hands of a Sherman tank squadron from 4th Armoured Brigade. The Italian force retreated with heavy casualties. The British/Canadian 30th Corps, advancing farther inland, faced less serious opposition, although they did clash with elements of the Divisione Napoli.

The Royal Navy was anxious to secure the Syracuse and Augusta ports and had been repeatedly probing the port defenses with the intention to land special forces at the earliest opportune moment. They were rebuffed on several occasions by Italian coastal batteries but, on the afternoon of July 12, there were reports of a white flag flying from the Augusta citadel. The SAS Special Reconnaissance Squadron was embarked on the landing ship *Ulster Monarch* and sent into Augusta harbor with three escorting destroyers. The convoy came under fire from Italian coastal batteries still active on Cape Santo Croce north of the port, and these were silenced by the destroyers. The SAS force disembarked from landing craft around 1925hrs and found the port largely deserted. They bumped into patrols from Kampfgruppe Schmalz on the outskirts of the port but, before a major confrontation developed, the Germans retreated in the face of the advancing 17th Brigade columns.

The absence of serious resistance on the British invasion beaches and the embarrassing disintegration of the PMM Siracusa-Augusta stronghold led to bitter recriminations between the Italians and the Germans. The abysmal communication between German and Italian units during the several counterattacks left the Germans with the mistaken impression that the Italians had failed to put up a fight anywhere in this sector.

THE INITIAL AXIS RESPONSE: AIR OPERATIONS

Owing to the effectiveness of the pre-invasion Allied air operations, Axis strikes against the Allied naval forces off Sicily were far below the dire predictions of earlier Allied intelligence. The Superaero (Italian air force high command) had ordered a strike against the Western Task Force, consisting of a squadron of torpedo bombers from Sardinia and a P.108 heavy bomber squadron from Perugia, which hit the Cent Force off Scoglitti in the pre-dawn hours before being driven off by anti-aircraft fire and Spitfires. Around the same time, another air attack struck the Dime Force off Gela, and the destroyer *Maddox* was sunk around dawn by a Ju-88 bomber of KG 54. The minesweeper *Sentinel* was severely damaged moments later. Air attacks on the fleets occurred steadily through the day. Besides the high-altitude bombers, FW-190 fighter-bombers were active, including skip-bombing attacks against the LSTs off Gela; that evening they scored a hit against LST-313, knocking out one of the vital pontoon causeways feeding the Gela beachhead. Axis fighters based on Sicily constantly harassed the catapult seaplanes being used by the US Navy for artillery spotting along the landing beaches. Attacks on the British sectors were less effective, owing to more extensive fighter patrols, but the hospital ship *Talamba* was sunk. In total, Luftflotte 2 conducted 370 sorties on the first day and the Regia Aeronautica a further 141 missions. The air attacks

US Army military police inspect a Bf-109G of JG 53 that was shot down on July 10 while attempting to strafe the landing beaches. (NARA)

intensified on July 11, with 282 German and 198 Italian sorties; 19 aircraft were lost. The most spectacular naval casualty was the Liberty ship *Robert Rowan*; its load of ammunition cooked off after bomb strikes. Axis air attacks fell in volume over the following week, with 373 sorties on July 12 but only 161 by July 15. During the first six days of the campaign, Luftflotte 2 conducted 1,260 missions and the Regia Aeronautica another 871 sorties; Axis casualties were 146 aircraft in the air. On July 15, both Italian and German air units began to abandon bases on Sicily and move to the Italian mainland or Sardinia. As a result, the Axis air missions diminished greatly in the subsequent week, further constrained as Allied forces established fighter bases on Sicily. The USAAF began deploying fighters near Gela starting on July 12; the RAF began deploying Spitfires the following day from Pachino.

The beaches off Gela were the scene of several intense air attacks on July 10–11. This is the view from the cruiser USS *Boise* moments after the ammunition-laden transport ship *Robert Rowan* blew up in the late afternoon of July 11, after being hit by several bombs from Ju-88 bombers. (NARA)

AXIS REASSESSMENT

By the night of July 11–12, a clearer picture was emerging of the day's attempted counterattacks. In the eyes of both Guzzoni and Kesselring, the most alarming development was the collapse of the Syracuse defenses. Radio contact with the Augusta naval command had been lost, and there was only limited appreciation of the dangers there. Since early reports from Gela suggested that the American landings there had been defeated, the orders at the end of the day instructed the Panzer-Division "Hermann Göring" to shift toward Syracuse to block the British advance on Catania and Messina. In spite of Divisione Livorno's crippling losses on July 11, the unit was ordered to change the orientation of its attacks and block the US 3rd Division in the Licata sector. As further reports flowed in that evening, the assessment began to darken; the Gela attacks had failed and the situation around Syracuse was disastrous. Generalleutnant Senger und Etterlin urged that plans be initiated to evacuate Sicily. Kesselring visited Sicily on July 12, and there was general agreement that the chance of eliminating the Allied bridgeheads was no longer possible after the defeats of the July 11 counterattacks. The best that could be hoped for was containment.

Mussolini was outraged by the reports of the abandonment of the Syracuse-Augusta naval base and asked for a frank assessment from the Comando Supremo. On July 14, Gen. Ambrosio reported that the fate of Sicily was already sealed and that the Allies would soon be able to invade the Italian mainland. So long as the Axis was tied down on the Eastern Front, there was no possibility for Axis victory. He urged that all Italian troops be withdrawn from Russia, the Balkans, and France to reinforce the Italian front. He concluded that Mussolini should "plan to end the war to spare the country from waste and destruction." He warned Mussolini a few days later that Germany wanted "to make Italy her battleground… as the outer defense line of the Reich."

The assessment of the situation in Berlin was no more sanguine. Reports from the Syracuse front reported widespread panic among the Italian forces and a general rout from the port. Hitler had lost what little confidence he had in his Italian allies and efforts began to ensure that tactical command of the defenses on Sicily come under German control. Hitler authorized the gradual transfer of 1. Fallschirmjäger-Division to Sicily, starting with the air transport of a regiment to the Catania Plains followed by land transport of the remainder of the division. The 29. Panzergrenadier-Division was notified

Axis air raids remained a persistent threat even after the first week of the campaign. The British beaches in eastern Sicily were periodically raided from bases in nearby Calabria. This British 40mm Bofors crew stands on guard, while in the background can be seen an Italian Macchi MC-202 fighter downed in an earlier raid. (NARA)

to prepare for movement to Sicily. To facilitate this process, Generaloberst Hans-Valentin Hube's XIV Panzer Korps headquarters in southern Italy was delegated with the task of taking over control of German units on Sicily.

As a result of the Sicily crisis, on July 13 Hitler decided to call off Operation *Zitadelle*, the offensive on the Kursk salient in Russia. The reason for this decision was not due to plans to transfer large forces from Russia to Sicily, but rather that the Italian performance on Sicily was a harbinger of Italian withdrawal from the war, which created an immediate need to build up a reserve force to replace the Italian army's 80 divisions. Some of the more pessimistic officers wanted immediate and drastic action. Admiral Dönitz recommended that the Kriegsmarine take over the Italian fleet rather than let it slip into Allied hands; likewise the Kriegsmarine should take control of major Italian naval bases "otherwise Taranto and Naples would meet the same fate as Augusta." But for the time being, Hitler sided with Kesselring's more optimistic view that the threat on Sicily could be contained long enough to provide a breathing spell for the Wehrmacht to prepare its future options in the Mediterranean. Hitler remained convinced that the Allies were still planning to strike in the Balkans and so was unwilling to commit resources to Sicily until the last moment.

On July 15, Mussolini met with Kesselring, Ambrosio, and other senior commanders to discuss future plans on Sicily. Kesselring wanted a new defensive line in front of Mount Etna to slow the Allied advance; Mussolini wanted the line farther west in the Madonie Mountains but he was ignored. Kesselring acknowledged plans to add 29. Panzergrenadier-Division to Axis forces on Sicily but Mussolini asked why 3. Panzergrenadier-Division in Tuscany couldn't moved to the Calabrian coast opposite Sicily. Kesselring knew full well that it was committed to the *Alarich* operation and he had to invent excuses.

Hitler and Mussolini met at Feltre near Venice on July 19. The Commando Supremo had hoped that the conference would initiate a conversation on how Italy could withdraw from the war without unduly harming German interests. Instead, Mussolini sheepishly refused to confront the Führer and endured one of Hitler's tedious two-hour monologues on the war situation. The disappointing results of the conference prompted senior Italian army commanders and high-ranking members of the Fascist party to call for a meeting of the Grand Council; sources close to the king hinted that his unquestioned support of Mussolini had disappeared. A slow coup was under way in Rome.

BEYOND THE YELLOW LINE

The defeat of the Axis counteroffensive on July 11 initiated a series of delaying actions to permit new defense lines to be erected to shield the evacuation sites along the Messina Straits. The 15. Panzergrenadier-Division's transfer into western Sicily was well under way, followed a few days later by the Aosta and Assieta divisions. The most critical point in the new defense line was Catania, since the plains southeast of Mount Etna presented the most immediate opportunity for the Allies to reach Messina. The Catania Plain was relatively flat and open, while the corridor north of Mount Etna was mountainous and easier to defend. While Hitler had decided for the moment to hold Sicily, there were few doubts among German commanders that evacuation was the eventual outcome.

THE BOMBER MENACE (pp. 58–59)

Land-based German and Italian bombers and torpedo-bombers were a significant threat to Allied naval forces in the 1940–43 Mediterranean campaigns. Based on Sicily, Pantelleria, and the Italian coast, these aircraft became an increasing menace with the advent of coastal surface-search radars, which could locate Allied shipping night or day in all weather and track the convoys. Forward Axis bases such as Pantellaria were a threat as much for their radar stations as their forward airbases. Following the *Husky* landings, Axis bombers in July sank one destroyer, one minesweeper, five landing ships, and seven cargo ships and auxiliaries (48,685 tons).

The illustration here shows one of the most common of the Axis bombers, the Luftwaffe's Junkers Ju-88A-4. It depicts an attack by elements of 7. Staffel of III./KG 54 on the afternoon of July 11 against the US beachheads in the Scoglitti–Gela area **(1)**. That afternoon, a large force numbering two to three dozen Ju-88s from I./KG 6 and III./KG 54 struck both the Cent and Dime beachheads. Around 1540hrs, they hit the Liberty ship *Robert Rowan* **(2)** with at least three bombs. The ship was loaded with ammunition and, when the firefighting effort proved to be of no avail, the crew abandoned ship. The ship exploded with

considerable force and burned close to the beach for most of the day.

The aircraft in the foreground (B3+GR) was piloted by Lt. Kurt Fox **(3)**. It had secured one of the first Luftwaffe victories of the Sicilian campaign during a dawn attack the day before on July 10. During the previous attack, one of its bombs struck under the starboard propeller guard of the destroyer DD-622 USS *Maddox*, detonating the aft magazine. Of her crew, 211 were lost and 74 were saved. The typical weapons load for the Ju-88 on these missions was the SC-250 250kg (550lb) high-explosive bomb.

The III./KG 54 "Totenkopf" was one of the most experienced Luftwaffe bomber *Gruppen* in the Mediterranean. The original unit of this designation had been formed in 1940 and had fought in France before being dissolved. In September 1942, K.Gr.806 based at Catania on Sicily was redesignated as III./KG 54. The Gruppe subsequently fought during the autumn 1942 convoy battles in the central Mediterranean, as well as attacks on Malta. In late 1942 and early 1943 it took part in the Tunisia fighting, and was eventually based at Grottaglia near Taranto in response to the Allied air attacks that preceded Operation *Husky*; it was commanded by Maj. Franz Zauner.

The Allies' tactical goal was to push the beachheads out to encompass the airfields contained within the "Yellow Line" objectives. In the American sector, the bulge created in the center against 1st Division around Gela was straightened out. On the far left flank, 3rd Division had made excellent progress, but Alexander was hesitant about it pushing farther west towards Agrigento, as he was concerned that the reports of Axis forces moving westward were the harbinger of further counterattacks from this sector. On the American right flank, the 45th Division met the 1st Canadian Division near Ragusa on July 12, creating a continuous Allied front line.

In the British sector, 13th Corps had secured Augusta on July 14, and the neighboring 30th Corps had pushed inland against very meager opposition. The primary objective for 8th Army beyond Augusta was the port of Catania and the extensive airfield complex at Gerbini. Montgomery was so optimistic about 8th Army's progress that he decided he could divide his forces, with 30th Corps moving rapidly around Mount Etna to Messina from the northwest while 13th Corps continued its advance up the Catania Plains. The new plans meant that 30th Corps would move westward along Highway 124 towards Caltagirone, even though this sector had been assigned to the Seventh US Army in the *Husky* plans. He informed Alexander of his plans without coordinating them with 15th Army Group headquarters. Montgomery's unilateral decision would prove to be one of the most controversial and consequential of the campaign. It was based on an overly optimistic assessment of the weakness of Axis forces to the northwest of Mount Etna, and presumed that 30th Corps could execute a rapid advance through the difficult mountain terrain against negligible opposition, while at the same time assuming that Catania was in easy grasp of 13th Corps. In addition to dispersing 8th Army's strength along two completely different axes of attack, Patton's substantial Seventh US Army was dismissed to the role of flank guard. As would transpire, Kesselring was able to establish defenses in front of 30th Corps faster than they could advance northward.

In the afternoon of July 13th, the 157th Infantry from 45th Division began bumping into the 51st Highland Division on the approaches to Vizzini, even though this portion of Highway 124 was in the American sector. Late that night Patton's headquarters received a directive from Alexander that

A 25-pdr of 7th Battery, 2nd Field Regiment, RCA conducts a fire mission during 1st Canadian Divisions' assault on Agira in late July 1943. (NARA)

61

adopted Montgomery's plan from earlier in the day; the Americans would cede Highway 124 and the immediate approaches north to Etna to the British 30th Corps. Without the western part of Highway 124, the 45th Division would have to withdraw back to the beaches in order to shift westward. The II Corps commander, Omar Bradley, was livid over the unexpected change and felt that it reflected Alexander's continuing lack of confidence in the US Army's combat effectiveness. This incident would strongly color his future views of Montgomery. Patton was somewhat more restrained in his reactions, but he already had begun to consider other options for Seventh US Army, eyeing the original objective of Palermo. If Montgomery could set his own agenda, then so could Patton.

While this controversy was developing, Montgomery's 13th Corps was conducting a series of bold adventures to push through Kampfgruppe Schmalz toward Catania. The Catania Plain was repeatedly intersected by rivers flowing off Etna and their associated ravines. The plan was to seize two key bridges at Lentini and Primosole using special forces in advance of the main 13th Corps assault. No. 3 Commando disembarked from landing craft near Agnone on the coast at 2200hrs on July 13 and marched inland to the Melati bridge. The teams removed the demolitions from the bridge and waited for the advance of 50th Division, which was expected to arrive around 0430hrs on July 14. But the 13th Corps advance was held up by fighting around Lentini with Kampfgruppe Schmalz. No. 3 Commando was obliged to give up the bridge in the face of a counterattack by Ten. Col. Tropea's Gruppo Tattico "Carmito"; the commandos dispersed back towards friendly lines.

The capture of the hill town of Centuripe by 38 Brigade, 78th Division on August 3 was a key step in the Operation *Hardgate* advance on Adrano. Here, a British patrol goes house to house to check for any remaining German troops. (NARA)

Beach-head breakout, July 13–18, 1943

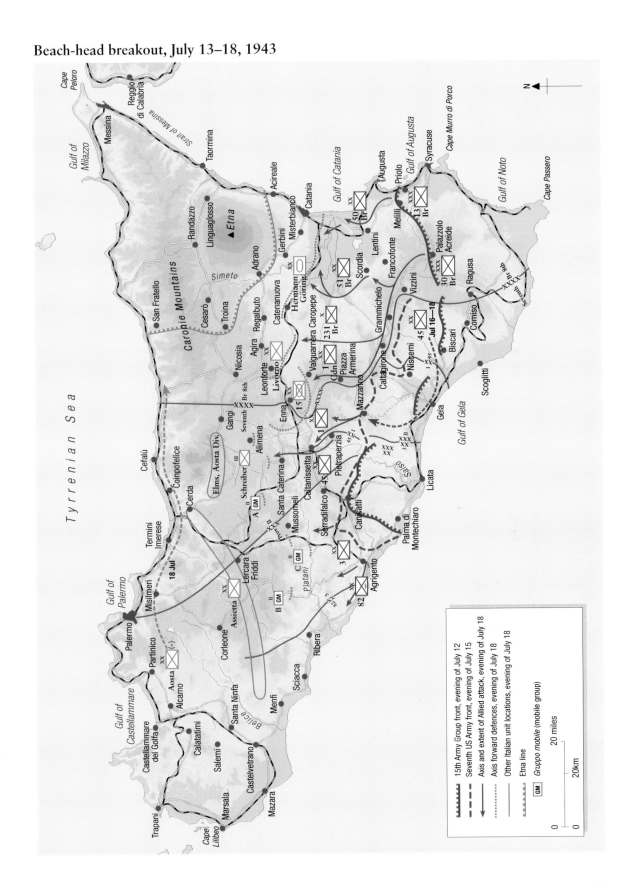

A PzKpfw IV Ausf. G of 3./ Panzer-Abteilung 215, 15. Panzergrenadier-Division, knocked out during the fighting with the Canadian 1st Division on the road between Agira and Regelbuto during the Operation *Hardgate* offensive. (National Archives Canada PA-130377)

The deeper paratroop mission, codenamed *Fustian*, was aimed at securing the Primosole bridge over the Simeto river farther up the coast using troops of 1st Parachute Brigade. In view of the disastrous *Husky 2* mission the previous day, the flight path from Tunisia to the drop zone was designed to skirt around the Allied fleets, but the initial flights came under fire from both the Allied fleet and Axis shore batteries. Of the original 105 C-47s, only 39 planeloads of paratroopers landed within a mile of the intended drop zones and only about 200 of the 1,900 British paratroopers who jumped on the night of July 13 reached the bridge before midnight. The bridge area was defended by the Italian 372° Rgt. costiere, as well as a heavy weapons battalion of the German 1. Fallschirmjäger-Division that had air-landed at Catania airfield that afternoon.

A column of Sherman III tanks supporting 1st Canadian Division enter the shattered remains of the hill town of Regalbuto on August 3 during Operation *Hardgate* in the course of the fighting against Fallschirmjäger-Regiment 3. This attack was part of a two-pronged effort by 13th Corps, along with the capture of Centuripe to the east, to seize the key road junction of Adrano at the foot of Mt Etna. (NARA)

The British paratroopers quickly won control of the bridge as well as some adjacent hills, but soon came under attack from the German paratroopers south of the bridge. By dawn, there were about 295 British paratroopers at Primosole bridge. They were able to hold off Axis attacks from both sides of the bridge through most of the day with the help of naval gunfire. Casualties at the bridge increased and ammunition finally ran out, forcing the paratroopers to withdraw south around 1830hrs to defensive positions in the hills south of the bridge.

Lead elements of 50th Division finally reached the Melati bridge near Lentini around 1700hrs on July 14, and fought their way through German rearguards during the day. They reached positions about a mile from the British paratroopers at Primosole by nightfall when they halted. The paratroopers met up with 50th Division early on July 15 and resumed the attacks on the bridge, which by this stage had been reinforced. The Germans attempted to demolish the bridge using trucks carrying explosives, but this was unsuccessful. After two costly days of fighting, the British infantry outflanked the defenses over the Simeto Rriver and finally recaptured the Primosole bridge on July 16. By this time, the bridge had lost its value as the Germans had established far more formidable defenses on the approaches to Catania.

After fighting a long series of delaying actions against pursuing American, British, and Canadian units, the rest of Panzer-Division "Hermann Göring" and the remnants of Divisione Livorno pulled back over the Simeto Rriver on July 15 to reinforce further the defensive lines in front of Catania. Likewise, 15. Panzergrenadier-Division had already moved from western Sicily and was prepared to defend the northwestern approaches to Messina above Mount Etna against 30th Corps. Generalabat Hube arrived on Sicily on July 15 to establish the XIV Panzer Korps headquarters. Although Guzzoni remained in nominal command, direction of the fighting on the eastern side of Mount Etna on the Catania Plains was left to the Germans under Hube while Gen. Arisio's XII Corpo was responsible for the northwestern approaches. Oberst Baade, who had earlier been involved in the formation of 15. Panzergrenadier-Division on Sicily, was assigned the new task of reinforcing the Messina Straits with flak and coastal artillery in anticipation of an eventual evacuation effort.

After weeks of fighting, on August 5 the British 78th Division of 30th Corps finally secured the key road junction of Adrano on the approaches to Messina along the northern route.

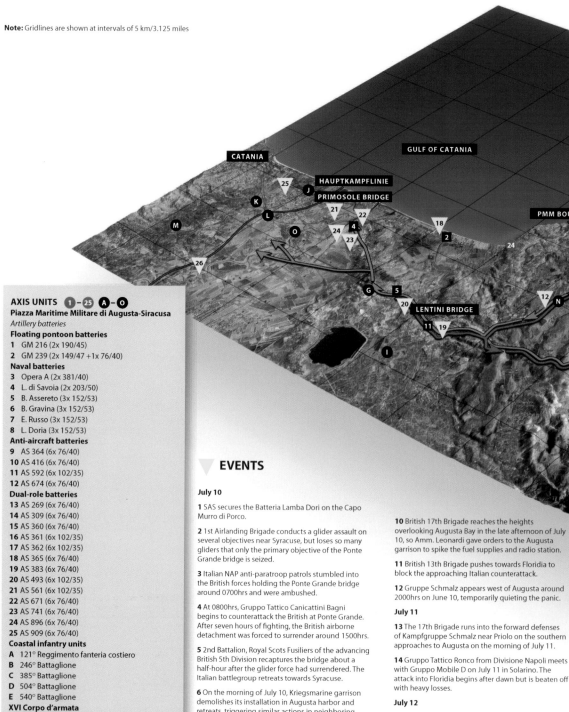

Note: Gridlines are shown at intervals of 5 km/3.125 miles

CATANIA

GULF OF CATANIA

HAUPTKAMPFLINIE

PRIMOSOLE BRIDGE

PMM BOUNDARY

LENTINI BRIDGE

AXIS UNITS ①–㉕ Ⓐ–Ⓞ
Piazza Maritime Militare di Augusta-Siracusa
Artillery batteries
Floating pontoon batteries
1 GM 216 (2x 190/45)
2 GM 239 (2x 149/47 +1x 76/40)
Naval batteries
3 Opera A (2x 381/40)
4 L. di Savoia (2x 203/50)
5 B. Assereto (3x 152/53)
6 B. Gravina (3x 152/53)
7 E. Russo (3x 152/53)
8 L. Doria (3x 152/53)
Anti-aircraft batteries
9 AS 364 (6x 76/40)
10 AS 416 (6x 76/40)
11 AS 592 (6x 102/35)
12 AS 674 (6x 76/40)
Dual-role batteries
13 AS 269 (6x 76/40)
14 AS 309 (6x 76/40)
15 AS 360 (6x 76/40)
16 AS 361 (6x 102/35)
17 AS 362 (6x 102/35)
18 AS 365 (6x 76/40)
19 AS 383 (6x 76/40)
20 AS 493 (6x 102/35)
21 AS 561 (6x 102/35)
22 AS 671 (6x 76/40)
23 AS 741 (6x 76/40)
24 AS 896 (6x 76/40)
25 AS 909 (6x 76/40)
Coastal infantry units
A 121° Reggimento fanteria costiero
B 246° Battaglione
C 385° Battaglione
D 504° Battaglione
E 540° Battaglione
XVI Corpo d'armata
F Gruppo Tattico Canicattini Bagni
G Gruppo Mobile D
H Gruppo Tattico Ronco
I Gruppo Tattico "Carmito"
J 372° Reggimento costiere
K 162° Gruppo artiglieria (149/35)
L 165° Gruppo artiglieria (149/35)
M 275° Gruppo artiglieria (305/17)
N Kampfgruppe Schmalz
O Heavy weapons battalion, 1. Fallschirmjäger-
   Division

▼ EVENTS

July 10

1 SAS secures the Batteria Lamba Dori on the Capo Murro di Porco.

2 1st Airlanding Brigade conducts a glider assault on several objectives near Syracuse, but loses so many gliders that only the primary objective of the Ponte Grande bridge is seized.

3 Italian NAP anti-paratroop patrols stumbled into the British forces holding the Ponte Grande bridge around 0700hrs and were ambushed.

4 At 0800hrs, Gruppo Tattico Canicattini Bagni begins to counterattack the British at Ponte Grande. After seven hours of fighting, the British airborne detachment was forced to surrender around 1500hrs.

5 2nd Battalion, Royal Scots Fusiliers of the advancing British 5th Division recaptures the bridge about a half-hour after the glider force had surrendered. The Italian battlegroup retreats towards Syracuse.

6 On the morning of July 10, Kriegsmarine garrison demolishes its installation in Augusta harbor and retreats, triggering similar actions in neighboring Italian detachments.

7 The coastal infantry battalions defending the ports retreat prior to contact with British forces. During the afternoon, the coastal batteries begin spiking their guns.

8 The Royal Navy repeatedly probes the port defenses of Augusta with the intention to land special forces at the earliest opportune moment.

9 The gun batteries on Capo Santo Panagia, including the massive guns of the Opera A battery, open fire on Royal Navy ships probing Augusta harbor; these batteries hold out until dawn on July 11.

10 British 17th Brigade reaches the heights overlooking Augusta Bay in the late afternoon of July 10, so Amm. Leonardi gave orders to the Augusta garrison to spike the fuel supplies and radio station.

11 British 13th Brigade pushes towards Floridia to block the approaching Italian counterattack.

12 Gruppe Schmalz appears west of Augusta around 2000hrs on June 10, temporarily quieting the panic.

July 11

13 The 17th Brigade runs into the forward defenses of Kampfgruppe Schmalz near Priolo on the southern approaches to Augusta on the morning of July 11.

14 Gruppo Tattico Ronco from Divisione Napoli meets with Gruppo Mobile D on July 11 in Solarino. The attack into Floridia begins after dawn but is beaten off with heavy losses.

July 12

15 On the afternoon of July 12, the SAS Special Reconnaissance Squadron on the landing ship *Ulster Monarch* steams into Augusta harbor with three escorting destroyers.

16 The SAS convoy comes under fire from Italian coastal batteries still active on Cape Santo Croce north of the port; these are silenced by the destroyers.

17 The SAS force disembarks from landing craft around 1925hrs and finds the port largely deserted. They bump into patrols from KG Schmalz on the outskirts of the port but, before a major confrontation develops, the Germans withdraw when confronted by the advancing 17th Brigade columns.

PMM
Augusta -Siracusa
LEONARDI

KG
Schmalz
SCHMALZ

BRITISH UNITS **1** - **11**
8th Army
1 SAS Special Reconnaissance Squadron
2 No. 3 Commando
3 1st Airlanding Brigade
4 1st Parachute Brigade
13th Corps
5 4th Armoured Brigade
5th Division
6 2nd Battalion, Royal Scots Fusiliers
7 13th Brigade
8 15th Brigade
9 17th Brigade
50th Division
10 69th Brigade
11 151st Brigade

AUGUSTA

GULF OF AUGUSTA

SYRACUSE

PONTE GRANDE

FLORIDIA

13
Br
DEMPSEY

July 13

18 No. 3 Commando disembarks from landing craft near Agnone on the coast at 2200hrs on July 13 and seizes the Melati bridge.

19 Kampfgruppe Schmalz stymies 13th Corps advance around Lentini.

20 Gruppo Tattico "Carmito" counterattacks No. 3 Commando, which disperses back towards friendly lines.

21 On the night of July 13, 1st Parachute Brigade conducts Operation *Fustian* to secure the Primosole bridge. Only 39 planeloads of paratroopers land within a mile of the drop zones and only about 200 of the 1,900 British paratroopers who jump reach the bridge before midnight.

July 14

22 After a day of intense fighting, casualties and shortage of ammunition force the paratroop detachment at the bridge to withdraw into the hills south around 1830hrs.

23 Lead elements of 50th Division reach the Melati bridge near Lentini around 1700hrs on July 14 and push on to within a mile of the British paratroopers at Primosole by nightfall when they halt.

July 15

24 The paratroopers meet up with 50th Division early on July 15. The Germans attempt to demolish the bridge using trucks carrying explosives, but this is unsuccessful.

July 16

25 British infantry outflanks the defenses over the Simeto River and finally recapture the Primosole bridge on July 16.

26 Kampfgruppe Schmalz, reinforced by elements of 1. Fallschirmjäger-Division, establishes strong blocking positions in front of Catania as part of the Hauptkampflinie. The positions are backed by significant Italian artillery.

BATTLE FOR THE CATANIA GATEWAY
British Special Forces lead the way on the approaches to Catania, July 10–18

The solidification of German defenses in front of Catania encouraged Montgomery to place more focus on the northern approaches to Messina and, in a clarification of the July 13 directive, Alexander allotted three of the four routes into Messina to 8th Army while leaving Patton's Seventh US Army to secure Montgomery's western flank against a phantom western threat. In the meantime, Patton had taken advantage of Alexander's permission to conduct a reconnaissance towards Agrigento to seize the port, providing a take-off point for the greater prize of Palermo on the northern coast. Palermo had been the original objective of Seventh US Army in the initial *Husky* plans, and would provide a substantial addition to Allied port capacity. On July 17, Patton visited Alexander in Tunisia and argued that an advance on Palermo was a superior method of guarding Montgomery's flank. Alexander reluctantly agreed, still skeptical of American capabilities.

THE RACE FOR PALERMO

Seventh US Army was awkwardly organized with only a single subordinate corps headquarters so, for the Palermo mission, Patton assigned his deputy commander, Maj. Gen. Geoffrey Keyes, to lead the Provisional Corps. Bradley's II Corps, already serving as a flank guard to the British/Canadian 30th Corps, remained in that thankless role and continued the advance up through the mountains into central Sicily.

On July 17, Arisio's 12° Corpo had been instructed to withdraw to establish new defense lines north of Mount Etna. It used its three mobile groups (Gruppi Mobile A, B, C) as rearguards to shield the withdrawal, and these were largely destroyed in the process. The Aosta and Assietta infantry divisions lost about 25–30 percent of their strength during the withdrawal, which was largely completed by July 22. In the process, western Sicily was stripped of its most capable units.

The spearhead for Keyes' Provisional Corps was the 504th Parachute Infantry, which started the 100-mile race on July 19. When the paratroopers gained 25 miles on the first day, Patton decided to accelerate the movement

Troops from the 45th Division advance along the coastal highway near Finale on July 28 during the fighting towards Santo Stefano. (NARA)

using 2nd Armored Division and Darby's Force X. The next day's advance bagged 4,000 Italian prisoners and, in parallel, 3rd Division moved on foot using its "Truscott Trot" training. By July 22, both 2nd Armored Division and 3rd Division were on the outskirts of Palermo. Like Syracuse-Augusta, Palermo was defended by substantial coastal defenses, but the garrison showed little will to fight. Generale Giuseppe Molinero surrendered the garrison at the royal palace that evening. The following day, 82nd Airborne Division was ordered to capture the port of Trapani while other ports were occupied by elements of 2nd Armored Division and Force X. In five days, the Provisional Corps suffered only 272 casualties; Italian casualties were 2,900 killed or wounded and 53,000 prisoners, though the prisoner count was undoubtedly low as the US Army encouraged "self-demobilization" of the demoralized Italian coastal divisions. The harbor at Palermo was clogged by sunken and scuttled vessels but US engineers had it operating at 30 percent capacity by July 28, when the first supply ships arrived. It became the primary supply center for Seventh US Army's new mission towards Messina.

THE FALL OF MUSSOLINI

The Fascist Grand Council met on the evening of July 24, voting against Mussolini's continued rule. When Mussolini visited Victor Emmanuel on July 25, he suggested that he would not voluntarily resign; the king insisted he resign and indicated that Maresciallo Pietro Badoglio had already been chosen to take his place. The reaction on the streets of Rome was an exuberant outpouring of gratitude to the king owing to the assumption that Italy would finally be free of this unpopular war. Unfortunately, neither the king nor Comando Supremo had made any firm decisions about how best to extricate Italy from the Berlin–Rome alliance.

When Berlin first learned of the coup, Hitler planned an immediate military action to take control of Italy, perhaps even to kidnap the royal family. Kesselring met with Badoglio and Ambrosio in Rome on July 26 and received assurances that Italy planned to abide by the Axis alliance, and his report to Berlin led to a temporary suspension of military measures. Nevertheless, Hitler suspected duplicity on the part of the Italians and the OKW drew up another plan, codenamed *Achse* (Axis), outlining a Wehrmacht operation to take control of Italy. Hitler's suspicions were sound as a week later the king approved a secret diplomatic mission to Portugal to contact British officials to discuss an armistice. While it would take weeks of negotiations before Italy withdrew from the war, by early August it was clear to senior Allied officials that the main objective of the Sicily operation was well in hand.

Victor and vanquished. Major-General Geoffrey Keyes, to the right, was Patton's deputy and commanded the Provisional Corps that captured Palermo. To his left is the Italian commander of the Palermo garrison, Generale di Brigata Giuseppe Molinero. (NARA)

Patton's race to Palermo, July 19–23

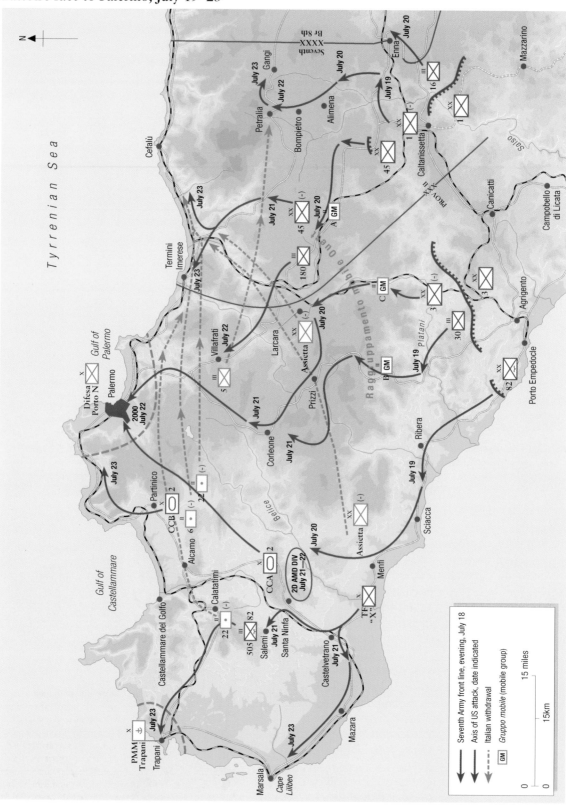

The immediate tactical outcome of the coup was a weakening of Hitler's resolve to hold Sicily in favor of reinforcing Wehrmacht strength in metropolitan Italy to deal with future contingencies. On July 26, Hitler informed Kesselring that preparations should begin for an eventual evacuation, but he later reconsidered these instructions and the evacuation was delayed pending further developments. Kesselring was determined to avoid repeating the Tunisian debacle and instructed Hube and Baade to continue preparations for an evacuation.

CONTAINING THE ALLIES

With 8th Army's advance up the Catania corridor stalemated by July 17 at the Primosole bridge, Montgomery hoped that 30th Corps might reach Messina less directly around the northern shoulder of Mount Etna via Randazzo. On July 21, Montgomery reinforced the northern push by bringing over his reserve division, the British 78th Division, from North Africa. However, Axis reinforcement of the northern front substantially outweighed these efforts as part of Kesselring's scheme for containment.

The Catania Plain was guarded primarily by Panzer-Division "Hermann Göring", substantially reinforced by regiments of 1. Fallschirmjäger-Division and Italian artillery units. Divisione Livorno continued to shield the division's northwestern flank in the western foothills of Mount Etna. By mid-July, 15. Panzergrenadier-Division was effectively blocking the 1st Canadian Division, the left wing of 30th Corps. The 29. Panzergrenadier-Division was the last of the German reinforcements sent to Sicily prior to the coup against

The mountainous area northwest of Mount Etna was well suited to defense, as illustrated by this view from the American sector on August 7, 1943, showing how a single 88mm Flak gun had effectively blocked the single mountain road through this area. (NARA)

Mussolini and completed its deployment to the northern coast on July 25. The Aosta and Assietta divisions also withdrew into this sector, so the northern corridor to Messina via Randazzo was covered by two German and three Italian divisions in ideal defensive terrain.

In contrast to the first week of fighting along the coast, the combat in central and northern Sicily was fundamentally different. The mountainous terrain favored the defenders since the poor road network was easily interdicted. The roads frequently funneled through towns with old stone buildings, which could be converted into strongholds. In addition, the roads were nearly always overlooked by mountains, where the Axis forces could establish forward artillery observers. Although the Italian infantry units were of declining value in the final weeks of the campaign, the Italian artillery units were stalwart and there were good relations between these units and the German units they were supporting. Once away from the coast, the Allies lacked the earlier advantages of naval gunfire. The Germans had to be forced out of the mountain strongholds with infantry, one shattered Sicilian village after another.

The Seventh US Army race to Palermo had been accompanied by a parallel thrust by Bradley's II Corps to reach the northern Highway 113 coastal road near Termini Imerese. The 45th Division reached the coast on July 23, while 1st Division moved up to its east with hopes of reaching Cefalu on the coastal road. This advance was halted by a major change in Allied planning. In view of the slow pace of the 8th Army advance on both axes, Montgomery realized that 30th Corps could not open the northern corridor to Randazzo alone. With western Sicily cleared by Patton's race for Palermo, and with Bradley's II Corps already starting to establish a strong American presence on the Allied left flank, on July 23 Alexander changed plans. Patton's Seventh US Army was given the new operational objective of advancing toward Messina along two axes, the Highway 113 coastal road and the Highway 120 route through Randazzo. While not explicitly saying so, Alexander's new instructions initiated a race for Messina by Patton's and Montgomery's field armies.

The fight for Troina was one of the most costly of the Sicily campaign as the centerpiece of the defensive line of 15. Panzergrenadier-Division. This is a view looking from Cerami towards Troina on the ridge beyond, with Mount Etna in the background. (NARA)

At the same time, the Allied order of battle began to adjust for other new assignments. The Combined Chiefs of Staff had been reluctant to establish new objectives beyond Sicily until it was clear whether the Italian army would fight. Had the Italian army resisted more strongly on Sicily, Allied planners would have leaned toward operations against Sardinia or Corsica. In the event, the performance of the Italian army on Sicily had generally been poor and, with Mussolini's abdication, Italian resistance was expected to decline. Under these circumstances, bolder plans against mainland Italy were activated. Operation *Baytown*, a hasty British landing on the Italian "boot" was scheduled to follow the Allied conquest of Sicily, followed by the more substantial Operation *Avalanche* landing at Salerno a month after. Since these missions would be conducted with troops already in theater, some shuffling of the forces on Sicily ensued. Patton pulled both the 45th Division and 82nd Division out of the line for Salerno while substituting the 9th Division from North Africa. The British 5th Division and Canadian 1st Division were earmarked for *Baytown*.

The arrival of Hube's XIV Panzer Korps headquarters marked a steady shift in tactical control from the Italian to the German side. As early as July 22, Hube suggested that Guzzoni relinquish overall command on Sicily to the new headquarters, but Guzzoni refused. When Bradley's troops pushed north on July 23, it was becoming evident that the Allies would conduct a march on Messina on a third axis along the coastal route. Hube had little confidence in the Italian divisions along the HKL (Hauptkampflinie:main line of resistance) and was convinced that German units would have to take over the burden of Sicily's defenses. On July 25, Hube and Guzzoni agreed that XIV Panzer Korps would take over command on both sides of Mount Etna. As a sop, the Italians were delegated to defend the coast against Allied seaborne incursions. Following Mussolini's fall later that day, the Germans noted that the morale of Italian troops on Sicily plummeted. Through the last week of July, the three Italian divisions were absorbed piecemeal into neighboring German divisions. So for example, when the 1st Canadian Division captured Agira from 15. Panzergrenadier-Division on July 27–28, about a third of the troops captured there were Italians from the Divisione Livorno.

Following Alexander's July 23 directive, Bradley's II Corps began its hard struggle eastward from the Madonie mountain range towards the Caronie range. These mountain ranges were nearly impassable, so the corps was forced to fight along two narrow corridors, with 45th Division fighting along the coast road and 1st Division fighting down the narrow valleys to reach Randazzo. A key defensive position was the town of Nicosia astride the main route eastward. Fighting between 1st Division and elements of 15. Panzergrenadier-Division took nearly four days of bitter mountain fighting. On the evening of July 27 Hube authorized a withdrawal, part of a coordinated effort to pull back gradually to the Etna Line to shield Messina.

Montgomery and Bradley met Alexander at his new 15th Army Group headquarters at Cassible on July 25 to establish plans for an August offensive to push past Mount Etna. By this stage, Montgomery had largely given up hope of pushing through Catania, but he planned a feint by 13th Corps in this direction to distract the Germans. The main effort in early August was the Operation *Hardgate* offensive by 78th Division and the Canadian 1st Division toward Adrano. Bradley wanted to refresh his units after both 45th Division and 1st Division had taken a battering in the vicious mountain

The shift north of Etna, July 23, 1943

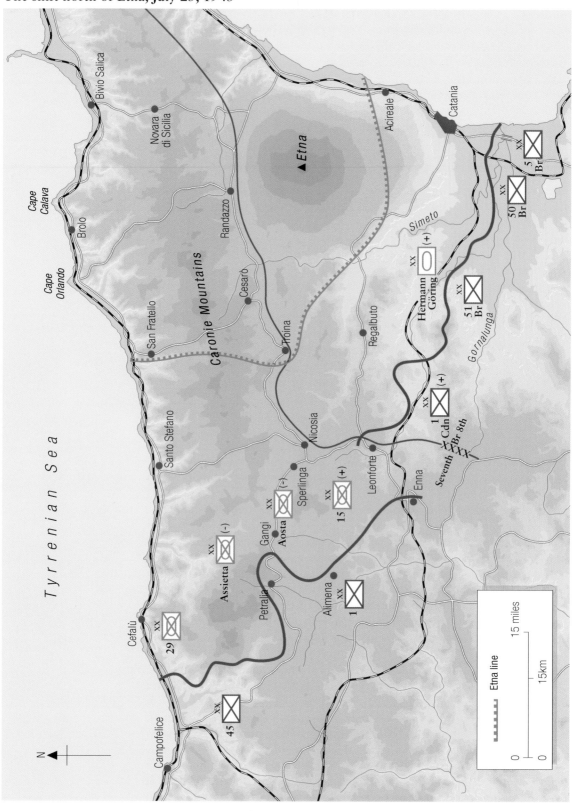

Etna

Catania

Acireale

Simeto

Gornalunga

xx
5 Br

xx
50 Br

xx
Hermann Göring (+)

xx
51 Br

xx
1 Cdn (+)

Regalbuto

XXXX
Seventh 8th

Nicosia

Enna

Leonforte

Sperlinga

xx
Aosta (-)

xx
15 (+)

xx
Assietta (-)

Gangi

Petralia

Alimena

xx
1

Cesarò

Troina

Randazzo

Caronie Mountains

San Fratello

Santo Stefano

Cefalù

xx
29

xx
45

Campofelice

Novara di Sicilia

Bivio Salica

Brolo

Cape Calava

Cape Orlando

Tyrrenian Sea

N

Etna line

15 miles

15km

0   0

74

Task Force Bernard from 2/30th Infantry staged an amphibious landing behind the lines of Panzergrenadier-Regiment 71 in the early morning hours of August 11 on the beach in front of Brolo, seen here to cut the coastal road. During the day, the retreating German columns overwhelmed the American positions on the beach and the remaining infantry companies took up positions in the foothills of Mount Cipolla, seen towards the top of this image. (NARA)

fighting of the previous week. The intention was to substitute the 3rd Division for the 45th Division on the coastal route facing 29. Panzergrenadier-Division, and 9th Division for 1st Division in the valleys heading on Highway 120 facing 15. Panzergrenadier-Division.

After regrouping from July 23 to 29, the British 30th Corps' *Hardgate* offensive proceeded on track, capturing Regalbuto and Centuripe on August 2–3 and opening the gateway to the main objective at Adrano. The American offensive also started on July 29, with the newly arrived 39th Infantry from 9th Division beginning an attack against the key road junction of Troina prior to the departure of 1st Division. Initial intelligence estimates expected Troina to be lightly held, but it became painfully evident that 15. Panzergrenadier-Division planned to hold the town as long as possible since it formed an obvious roadblock on the mountain route east. The 1st Division continued to deploy additional regiments into the fray and Troina proved to be one of the bloodiest battles of the Sicily campaign. The 15. Panzergrenadier-Division suffered 1,400 casualties, about 10 percent of its overall strength, but closer to 40 percent of its combat strength.

Hube did not wish to have his units consumed in attritional struggles, such as Troina and Catania, for fear that the units would be too weakened to take up new defense lines. The first garrison to withdraw was Panzer-Division "Hermann Göring" at Catania, which began its withdrawal on the night of August 4. This was followed by garrisons on the other side of Mount Etna, including Troina, on August 5.

The last German unit to withdraw was 29. Panzergrenadier-Division, reinforced by Divisione Assiette, which had been holding the San Fratello line on the coast in a bitter fight against the US 3rd Infantry Division since earlier in August. This rugged coastal area had been heavily fortified by the Italians in 1942–43. In order to break the stalemate, the 3rd Division staged an amphibious end run past the German defenses by leapfrogging the 2/30th Infantry up the coast using landing craft. The landing in the pre-dawn hours of August 8 surprised 2./Panzergrenadier-Regiment 71, but the landing occurred after the division had already executed most of its withdrawal.

Berlin delayed making a formal decision to abandon Sicily because Hitler and the OKW were focused on broader intrigues about Italy's fate. On August 6, German and Italian officials met at Travis to iron out issues relating to the transfer of German units into Italy. Both sides exchanged platitudes of fraternal goodwill, but in reality the OKW and Comando Supremo were engaged in a behind-the-scenes game of preparing for Italy's anticipated withdrawal from the war. The Italian army began shifting units to prevent a German seizure of Rome and the main naval base at La Spezia, while at the same time trying to confine the newly arrived German divisions to northern Italy.

While Berlin dithered, Kesselring took steps to ensure that the German forces on Sicily would not share the fate of their comrades in Tunisia. On August 2 he approved a detailed evacuation plan, leaving it to Hube's discretion when the various phases of the withdrawal should take place. The situation took a sudden turn for the worse on August 8. The American amphibious landing near San Fratello led to worries that further landings down the coast would cause the collapse of defenses on the northern coastal route. The two routes past the northern foothills of Mount Etna were threatened by the US 9th Division's capture of Cesaro and the British 78th Division capture of Bronte. The British 13th Corps, which had been stymied for weeks in front of Catania, had pushed 8 miles beyond the city. As a result, on August 8, Kesselring gave Hube formal permission to start the evacuation

Italians greet a British column from 17th Brigade, 5th Division, moving through Misterbianco in the suburbs of Catania on August 5. The armored vehicle is a Canadian-built Otter reconnaissance car. (NARA)

process. Guzzoni was informed of the decision on August 9 and the Comando Supremo ordered him to transfer his command to Calabria to head the defense efforts there. Guzzoni had already started the evacuation of idle Italian units from Messina on August 3, and this process accelerated after August 9.

The next defensive line, sometimes called the Tottorici Line, was activated on August 9–10 in another series of carefully executed retreats. One of the aims of this withdrawal was to pull the battered 15. Panzergrenadier-Division back toward the center, since it had already been earmarked as the first unit to be evacuated from Sicily. The withdrawing German forces made extensive use of demolitions to delay the Allied advance. Aside from obvious targets such as bridges and tunnels, the coastal roads and mountain passes also offered demolition opportunities. In turn, the Allied air forces attempted to stymie the German withdrawal with an air campaign against bridges and narrow passes. Allied air attacks on the critical withdrawal routes through Randazzo in the northern foothills of Mount Etna led to it being called the "death road" by 15. Panzergrenadier-Division. The road junction at Randazzo finally fell to a combined action by the US 9th Division and the British 78th Division on August 13.

Patton was intent on beating Montgomery into Messina and so focused his attention on the 3rd Division sector along the coastal Highway 113, which seemed more promising than the mountainous inland route. He decided to stage another amphibious leapfrog up the coast behind the Tottorici Line in the pre-dawn hours of August 11 to outflank the German defenses. Once again, Lt. Col. Lyle Bernard's task force from the 2/30th Infantry was assigned the mission. The landings put Task Force Bernard on the beaches immediately west of Brolo and the American infantry deployed to positions on Monte Cipolla overlooking the coastal road. Panzergrenadier Regiment 71 began a furious effort to overcome the roadblock before the rest of 3rd Division could link up with TF Bernard. By evening, the Germans overwhelmed the blocking elements of Bernard's forces along the coastal road. Naval support, including the cruiser *Philadelphia*, helped defend the

Catania, the key city on the road to Messina on the eastern side of Mount Etna, finally fell to the British 13th Corps on the morning of August 5 following the withdrawal of elements of the Panzer-Division "Hermann Göring" the night before. Here, a British patrol enters the shattered city. (NARA)

A column from the British 78th Division, outside Bronte on the road towards Randazzo, during the second week of August. Pack animals were essential in the fighting in the 30th Corps sector owing to the mountainous terrain and poor road conditions. (NARA)

beachhead, but the Luftwaffe sent repeated strikes against the ships. Through the night of August 11–12, the Germans withdrew their forces through Brolo. Bernard positioned his men for a "last stand" on the summit of Mount Cipolla but, in their rush to escape, Panzergrenadier-Regiment 71 largely ignored the defenders through the night. By morning, the lead elements of 3rd Division made their way to Bernard's beleaguered force.

On the night of August 11, the Germans began to evacuate 15. Panzergrenadier-Division across the Messina strait. Patton's lead units were still more than 50 miles from Messina; Montgomery's were more than 35 miles away.

The key road junction at Randazzo on the north side of Mount Etna was reached by Allied forces on August 13. Here, officers from the US 9th Division and British 78th Division meet outside the town. From left to right are Col. George Smith, 18th Infantry, Col. Paddy Flint, 39th Infantry, Maj. Gen. Vivian Evelegh, 78th Division, and Brig. E. E. E. Cass, 11th Brigade. (NARA)

Operation *Hardgate*, July 24–August 7, 1943

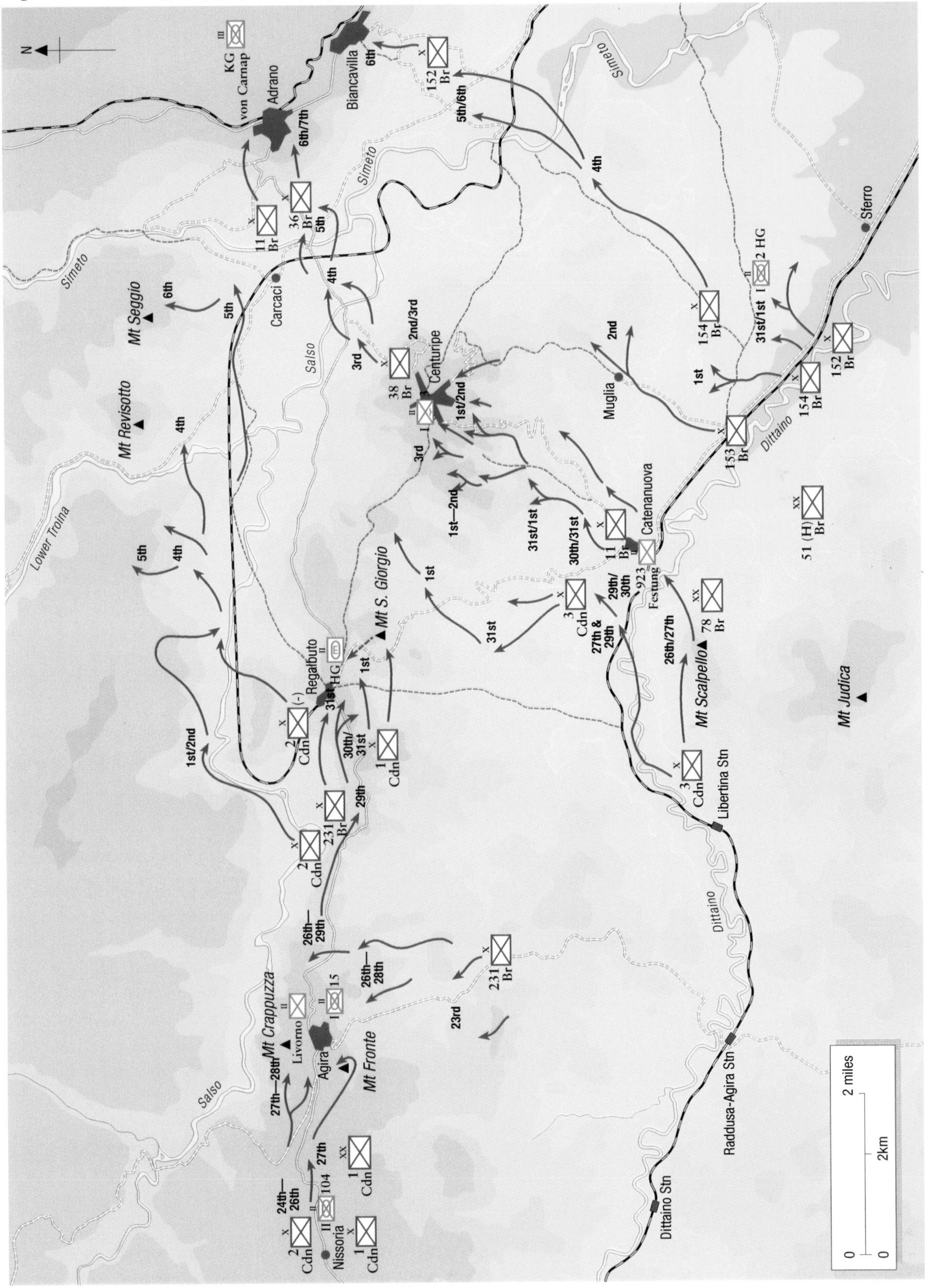

N

Adrano
von Carnap
KG
Biancavilla
6th
152
Br
5th/6th
6th/7th
36
Br
5th
11
Br
4th
5th
Mt Seggio
6th
Carcaci
4th
5th
Salso
3rd
2nd/3rd
Centuripe
38
Br
1st/2nd
3rd
Mt Revisotto
4th
1st—2nd
1st
2nd
Muglia
1st
154
Br
31st/1st
2 HG
Sferro
152
Br
154
Br
153
Br
Dittaino
Simeto
Simeto
4th
5th
4th
1st/2nd
Mt S. Giorgio
1st
31st/1st
30th/31st
11
Br
Catenanuova
923
Festung
29th/
30th
27th &
29th
3
Cdn
31st
26th/27th
Mt Scalpello
78
Br
51 (H)
Br
Mt Judica
Regalbuto
31st HG
1st
2
Cdn
30th
31st
1
Cdn
3
Cdn
Libertina Stn
Lower Troina
5th
4th
29th
2
Cdn
2 31
Br
3
Cdn
Dittaino
Raddusa-Agira Stn
26th—
29th
231
Br
26th
28th
23rd
Mt Crappuzza
27th—28th
Livorno
15
Agira
Mt Fronte
Salso
24th—
26th
27th
104
1
Cdn
2
Cdn
Nissoria
1
Cdn
Dittaino Stn

2 miles

2km

0

0

79

A 25-pdr battery from 13th Corps fires on positions of Panzer-Division "Hermann Göring" in the eastern foothills of Mount Etna near Zafferana during the final approach to Messina in the second week of August. (NARA)

OPERATION *LEHRGANG*

The German evacuation plan was codenamed Operation *Lehrgang* (Instruction Course). In late July, the crossing sites had been prepared under the direction of the inexhaustible Oberst Baade, who was named Kommandant Messina-Strasse (Commandant Messina Straits) on July 26. Baade concentrated on two major issues: collection of sufficient craft to conduct the evacuation and defense of the straits with both anti-aircraft guns and coastal batteries. Allied bombing had severely damaged existing ferry sites on the Straits, sinking many of the Italian ferries. However, the straits were quite narrow, only 2 miles at their narrowest point, and Baade was able to collect a variety of army and navy craft. Although most of the Italian train ferries had been knocked out by Allied air attacks, the Italian army used the surviving 932-ton *Villa* which was capable of carrying about 3,000 troops per voyage. This was supplemented by two steamboats and four navy motor rafts, and the Italian evacuation started a week before the German operation on August 3.

Baade took over command of the numerous Italian guns located in the PMM-Messina-Regio Calabria stronghold. This included 58 coastal gun batteries with over 150 guns on the Messina side of the straits, plus a further 66 antiaircraft gun batteries and 153 20mm antiaircraft guns. The Luftwaffe withdrew its 88mm gun batteries into this sector and Baade also commandeered divisional antiaircraft batteries to reinforce the site further. As of August 14, Baade had 333 anti-aircraft guns on both sides of the straits, though other records suggest that the total was closer to 500 guns.

In spite of the intense flak, the Allied air forces staged continual air attacks on the Messina area. Daylight missions from August 1 to 8 included 121 B-17 heavy bomber sorties and 225 RAF and USAAF fighter-bomber daylight sorties; the Wellington bombers conducted 269 sorties. The attacks intensified during the final ten days of the campaign with a total of 1,170 daylight sorties from August 8–17 and 442 night sorties by the Wellingtons on August 9–13. The Allied air forces claimed the destruction of 23 craft and damage on 43, though Axis records suggest the losses were far smaller. The small craft proved an elusive target, especially at night. Although Baade had planned to limit the evacuation to night runs across the straits, numerous daylight convoys were also conducted.

Axis evacuation from Sicily	Italy	Germany
Dates	Aug 3–16	Aug 11–16
Men	62,000*	39,569
Vehicles	300–500	9,605
Tanks	–	47
Artillery	75–100	94
Stores (tons)	–	17,000
Craft lost	8	7
Craft damaged	5	1

Italian sources vary; e.g. figures for troops are from 62,000 to 75,000

The Allied failure to stop the Axis evacuation became one of the most perplexing controversies of the Sicily campaign. Allied intelligence had reasonably sound information that an evacuation was planned, but there was a general failure of senior commanders to coordinate an effort to block the straits. Horatio Nelson once quipped that "A ship's a fool to fight a fort," and Adm. Cunningham was all too aware of the Royal Navy's debacle in the Dardanelles in March 1915, when several large warships were sunk by Turkish

The pursuit to Messina along the coast road was hampered by German demolitions. The most spectacular example was the destruction of a section of road at Cape Calava, with troops of 30th Infantry, 3rd Division gingerly walking over the rubble. The division's engineers created a temporary "bridge in the sky" to repair the gap, making it passable to light vehicle traffic. (NARA)

OPERATION *LEHRGANG* (pp. 82–83)

This illustration depicts a scene during the evacuation of Messina, codenamed Operation *Lehrgang*. The naval commander for this venture was the Seetransportführer Messina-Strasse, Kapitän Gustav von Liebenstein. He commanded the three Kriegsmarine transport flotillas on Sicily, Landungsflottillen 2, 4, and 10 and the similar army commands, including Landungs-Pionier-Battalion 771. Five army engineer battalions were also put at his disposal to prepare and operate the ferry points. At the time of Operation *Lehrgang*, Landungsflottille 2 had 20 navy ferry barges (MFP: *Marinefährprahm*) and two gun lighters (MAL: *Marine Artillerie-Leichte*), Landungsflottille 4 had additional MFP, and Landungsflottille 10 had a further ten Siebel ferries and ten small craft. The army engineers operated several Siebel ferries as well as landing barges (*Landungsboote*) and several dozen small boats (I-Boote: *Infanterieboote*). The Luftwaffe Flak forces in the area had additional Siebel ferries to provide floating air defense, and there were many smaller supplementary craft. This flotilla had the capacity to lift about 8,000 men and 2,000 metric tons of supplies and equipment per night. Escort was provided by an ex-French gunboat, the SG 14, and four 100-ton minesweepers.

The vessel in the foreground is a Siebel ferry (Siebelfähre) **(1)**, designed in 1940 by the aviation engineer Fritz Siebel as an expedient landing craft for the planned *Sea Lion* invasion of Britain. It was based on a pair of heavy bridge pontoons (*schwere Schiffsbrücke*) and powered with multiple automotive motors. They originally were constructed by the army in its Pionier-Sonderkommando (Engineer Special Command) in Antwerp. The concept was successful enough that it was taken up by the Luftwaffe and the Kriegsmarine. There was considerable variation in sizes and designs. The typical design had a displacement of 130 metric tons, a loaded speed of about 6–7 knots, and a capacity of about 50 metric tons and 150–250 troops. Some of the large designs had a capacity of up to 170 metric tons. They were often armed with 20mm Flak guns for self-defense, and some were converted into floating Flak batteries armed with 88mm guns.

While the Messina Straits flotilla is best known for the evacuation, it provided essential logistics support for the Axis during the Sicily campaign. From June through August, the units moved 59,579 men to Sicily, along with 13,489 vehicles and 29,619 metric tons of supplies. The flotilla suffered numerous losses to Allied air attack including at least four MFP, one Siebel ferry and eight smaller craft. In addition, seven MFP and two Siebel ferries were damaged.

The substantial Flak force deployed on either side of the Messina Straits greatly constrained Allied air attacks against the evacuation. This is an Italian Cannone-mitragliera Scotti 20/77 antiaircraft automatic cannon. There were 43 20mm batteries on Sicily, operated by the MACA (Milizia Volontaria artiglieria contraerea, 27 batteries) and the army (16 batteries). (MHI)

coastal defenses. The Royal Navy was well aware of the extent of Italian coastal artillery on both sides of the straits. The Allied navies were unwilling to risk their larger warships in the straits and believed that the air forces first should silence the coastal gun batteries. The air forces had little confidence that the numerous coastal artillery sites could be knocked out in the face of such intense flak and focused their attacks directly against the evacuation sites. Furthermore, the tactical air forces at the time were heavily committed to air support of the Allied ground forces and could not maintain a permanent presence over the straits, especially at night. The barges and craft used in the evacuation were small and fleeting targets, and transit for a ferry across the straits took only a half-hour. The problem was compounded by the widely scattered locations of the senior commanders, with Eisenhower and Tedder in North Africa, Alexander on Sicily, and Cunningham on Malta, which hampered coordination. Neither the Allied navies nor air forces were willing to endure heavy losses to stop the barge traffic and, lacking firm instructions from higher authorities, neither service really tried.

THE FINAL APPROACH TO MESSINA

On August 13, Panzer-Division "Hermann Göring" retreated from Taormina up Highway 114. The British 50th Division followed close on its heels but was delayed by extensive demolitions, booby traps, and minefields. From the other side of Mount Etna, the British 78th Division cleared the northern foothills of the volcano. The American advance on August 13 was swift since 29. Panzer-Division was withdrawing in haste after the scare at Brolo. Patton planned another leapfrog operation, this time reinforcing the amphibious task force with paratroopers. Major-General Truscott objected, fearing that it would occur so late that the landing force would be overtaken by his own units. In the event, the 157th Regimental Combat Team landed on the night of August 15–16 at Bivia Furnari, though by this time, Truscott's 3rd Division was already farther east on the coastal road. With the race for

Note: Gridlines are shown at intervals of 10 km/6.25 miles

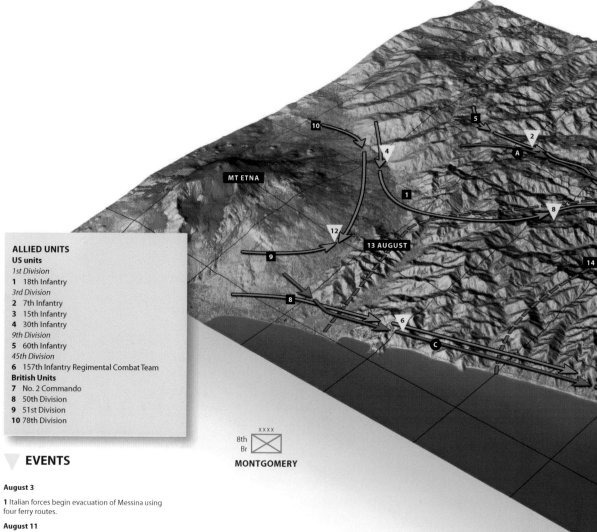

MT ETNA

13 AUGUST

14 A

8th
Br XXXX

MONTGOMERY

ALLIED UNITS
US units
1st Division
1 18th Infantry
3rd Division
2 7th Infantry
3 15th Infantry
4 30th Infantry
9th Division
5 60th Infantry
45th Division
6 157th Infantry Regimental Combat Team
British Units
7 No. 2 Commando
8 50th Division
9 51st Division
10 78th Division

▼ EVENTS

August 3

1 Italian forces begin evacuation of Messina using four ferry routes.

August 11

2 On the night of August 11–12, 15. Panzergrenadier-Division withdraws to Messina.

August 12

3 Plans to begin evacuation of 15. Panzergrenadier-Division on night of August 11–12 become delayed by communications problems and so begin during daylight hours.

August 13

4 The road junction at Randazzo falls to a combined action by the US 9th Division and the British 78th Division.

5 Elements of 3rd Division reaches Patti and push on towards Oliveri.

6 Panzer-Division HG retreat from Taormina, followed up Highway 114 by the British 50th Division, which was delayed by extensive demolitions, booby traps, and minefields.

August 14

7 3rd Division reaches Bivia Salica.

8 18th Infantry, 1st Division reaches Novara di Sicilia.

9 US columns from farther inland, including 60th Infantry, approach the coast.

August 15

10 A rearguard of Panzer-Division "Hermann Goring" holds up the British 50th Division at Scalletta through most of August 15.

11 7th Infantry, 3rd Division reaches Spadafora on the coast.

12 The British 13th and 30th Corps meet up on the northern side of Mount Etna near Linguaglossa.

13 The 157th Regimental Combat Team lands on the coast the night of August 15–16 at Bivia Furnari but the area has already been reached by 3rd Division.

14 The 29. Panzer-Division completes its evacuation to Calabria on night of August 15–16. The division's rearguards were about 200 men at Acqualadrone blocking the crossing site at the northeast tip of Sicily.

August 16

15 A force led by Brig. J. C. Currie from 4th Armoured Brigade with a half-squadron of tanks lands with Lt. Col. J. M. Churchill's No. 2 Commando at Cape d'Ali around 0430hrs on the morning of August 16.

16 A reinforced platoon of Co. L. 7th Infantry enters Messina on the evening of August 16–17.

August 17

17 The final elements of Panzer-Division "Hermann Goring" pull into the southern suburbs of Messina on the morning of August 17. The last German ferry headed over the Messina Straits in the pre-dawn hours of August 17, ending Operation *Lehrgang*.

18 Additional units of 7th Infantry enter Messina on the morning of August 17, along with at least a platoon from 157th Infantry.

19 30th Infantry pushes out to the northern tip of Sicily around Acqualadrone.

20 Around 0900hrs, the first British troops from Churchill's No. 2 Commando enter the city.

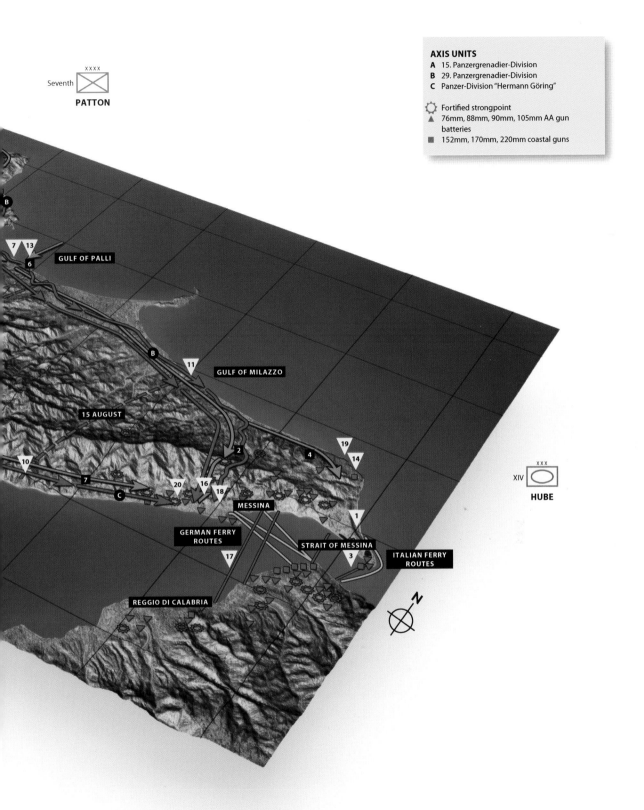

AXIS UNITS

A   15. Panzergrenadier-Division
B   29. Panzergrenadier-Division
C   Panzer-Division "Hermann Göring"

⬡   Fortified strongpoint
▲   76mm, 88mm, 90mm, 105mm AA gun batteries
■   152mm, 170mm, 220mm coastal guns

Seventh
XXXX
PATTON

7 13
6
GULF OF PALLI

B

11
GULF OF MILAZZO

15 AUGUST

2
4
19
14

XXX
XIV
HUBE

10
7
20 16
18
1

C

MESSINA

GERMAN FERRY ROUTES

STRAIT OF MESSINA

3

ITALIAN FERRY ROUTES

17

N

REGGIO DI CALABRIA

THE RACE TO MESSINA

The Axis succeed in evacuating a significant force across the Messina Straits

Messina in full swing, Montgomery decided on an amphibious landing as well, putting ashore a force at Cape d'Ali around 0430hrs on the morning of August 15, headed by Brig. J. C. Currie from 4th Armoured Brigade, with a half-squadron of tanks reinforcing Lt. Col. J. M. "Mad Jack" Churchill's No. 2 Commando.

On August 15, the German forces in front of Patton's Seventh US Army began to evaporate as it became time for 29. Panzer-Division to depart. The division completed its evacuation to Calabria on the night of August 15–16, except for small rearguards totaling 200 men. In the British sector, a rearguard of Panzer-Division "Hermann Göring" held up the British 50th Division at Scalletta through most of August 15. The final elements of this division were evacuated from Messina in the early morning hours of August 17, having halted Currie's column by demolishing a bridge over a deep ravine. The last German ferry headed over the Messina Straits in the pre-dawn hours of August 17, concluding Operation *Lehrgang*.

The first Allied troops to enter Messina was a reinforced platoon led by 1st Lt. Ralph Yates of Co. L. 7th Infantry on the evening of August 16–17. They were followed by additional units of 7th Infantry on the morning of August 17, along with at least a platoon from 157th Infantry. Around 0900hrs, the first British troops from Churchill's No. 2 Commando entered the city. Patton arrived at a ridge overlooking the city around 1000hrs and headed into Messina by staff car. Patton held a surrender ceremony in a park in the city center and, as it was concluding, Brig. Currie's Sherman tanks arrived. Patton shook hands and remarked "It was a jolly good race. I congratulate you."

Four Siebel ferries in Messina harbor prior to Operation *Lehrgang*. The evacuation was conducted from locations away from the main port owing to constant Allied air attacks. (NARA)

THE CAMPAIGN IN PERSPECTIVE

Axis losses during Operation *Husky* were severe, especially for the Italians. Total Italian losses were about 4,680 killed, 5,000 wounded, and about 152,000 missing or captured for a total of about 162,000. German losses were 4,561 killed, 4,583 missing, and 5,523 captured for a total of 14,667; a further 13,532 were wounded and evacuated for a grand total of about 28,000. The Germans lost 170 of 217 tanks and assault guns, while Italian AFV losses were total. Although Kesselring later boasted that the evacuated divisions were ready for service, this was a considerable exaggeration. The three principal German divisions involved in combat had lost well over half their effective combat strength in personnel and took months to rebuild. The Allies estimated Axis aircraft losses at 1,850 with some 1,421 wrecks being counted on Sicily after the fighting. The Regia Aeronautica acknowledged having 126 aircraft shot down and 286 lost in accidents or other non-combat causes. Allied losses were 2,237 killed and 5,946 wounded in the Seventh US Army, and 2,062 killed and 7,137 wounded in the British/Canadian 8th Army; Allied losses in naval units were 860 killed and 895 wounded.

Operation *Husky* succeeded in achieving its overall strategic goals of forcing Italy out the war, relieving pressure on the Red Army and opening the Mediterranean to maritime convoys. Following Mussolini's fall on July 25, the Italian government gingerly started negotiations with the Allies over

With a big smile on his face, Generaloberst Hans-Valentin Hube (left) is greeted by another German officer after arriving on the Calabrian coast near Campo Calabro at the end of Operation *Lehrgang*. (NARA)

LEFT
US troops enter the smoking ruins of Messina. A small patrol entered in the evening of August 16, with more substantial units the following day. (NARA)

RIGHT
The first British troops to enter Messina on August 17 were from No. 2 Commando. Some of them are seen having an impromptu lunch with some American troops that afternoon. (NARA)

an armistice, which was signed in secret on September 3 and officially announced on September 8, 1943. At the time of the armistice, the Italian armed forces had about 3.6 million men, of whom 2.6 million were in the army. There were a total of 82 Italian army divisions, of which about half were on occupation duty outside Italy, including southern France, Greece, Yugoslavia, and Russia. Hitler's forebodings about a possible Italian withdrawal from the war was his principal motive in calling a halt to the Kursk offensive in Russia on July 13. It was not only the loss of Italy that was the main source of his immediate misgivings, he was also anxious about the threat to the Balkans, as well as other potential weak points in Fortress Europe from the Mediterranean direction, such as the Adriatic coast near Leghorn and southern France. The sudden loss of the Italian divisions created an immediate gap in the defenses of the southern flank of Fortress Europe that could be addressed only by shifting resources from the Russian Front to the Mediterranean. From the peak Wehrmacht strength in Russia in the summer of 1943 of about 190 divisions, the forces there continually shrank to 185 at the end of 1943 and to about 160 by the summer of 1944, in spite of the growth of the opposing Red Army. German strength in the Balkans and Italy went from about 17 divisions in early 1943 to 24 immediately after the Sicily landings and 31 by the end of the year; Heeresgruppe G in southern France was expanded as well. While there were no German divisions permanently stationed in Italy in early 1943, by the summer of 1944 22 divisions were committed there.

Although the Axis managed to evacuate a substantial amount of equipment, a great deal remained behind in the Messina area including 78 armored vehicles, 287 artillery pieces, and about 3,500 vehicles. Here, US troops examine some of the Italian vehicles abandoned in Messina. (NARA)

From a tactical perspective, Sicily provided a mixed picture. On the one hand, the conduct of such an adventurous and complex amphibious landing operation was considerable evidence of the Allies' growing skills in combined operations. Likewise, the pre-landing intentions to win air superiority were clearly appreciated and well executed. The decision to conduct airborne operations at night without adequate navigation aids was a costly and amateurish mistake, though the airdrops on the first night were quite effective in disrupting Axis defenses. The conduct of the ground campaign was less impressive, in part owing to the cautious landing plan and concentration of all Allied forces in one sector. The deployment of both Allied field armies in southeastern Sicily proved troublesome once the beachheads were secured, since the terrain around Mount Etna channeled their advance along difficult and predictable routes. This allowed the modest Axis defensive forces to concentrate and delay the much larger Allied force. A dispersed landing at Palermo and Syracuse would have been riskier to conduct but would have complicated Axis defensive efforts. Although a great deal of ink has been spilled over the ego-driven controversies of the senior Allied commanders, these arguments are trivial compared to the dysfunctional Axis command structure. The failure to stop the Axis evacuation across the Messina Straits was an embarrassment, but it remains a mystery whether the Allies could have interrupted the barge traffic without enduring unacceptable warship losses to Axis coastal defenses.

The Italian performance on Sicily was not as poor as the Germans claimed, but neither was it particularly effective. The dismal performance of the coastal divisions and the naval strongholds has overshadowed the actions by the regular army formations and the air force. The Livorno division and the mobile groups fought bravely but were not well enough trained or equipped to prevail in their counterattacks. The Italian air force continued to conduct vigorous air operations through the campaign, in spite of the decrepit condition of much of their equipment.

Montgomery and Eisenhower on a plaza in Messina looking towards Calabria and the Italian mainland on August 30, 1943. Eisenhower later regretted not paying greater attention to the potential evacuation of Axis forces from Messina. (NARA)

THE BATTLEFIELD TODAY

There are numerous small traces of Operation *Husky*, but the 1943 campaign does not have the deep historical resonance of other events in Sicily's long history. The "Museo Storico dello Sbarco in Sicilia 1943" in Catania is the only museum dedicated to the campaign. It is a modern facility opened by the regional government in 2000 and containing many displays and exhibitions in the contemporary style with associated films and information displays. Several of the battlefield sites have small plaques or memorials, but they are not especially obvious in most cases. Monuments can be found dotted around the island in small numbers, predominantly commemorating incidents involving the Allied forces. There are hundreds of the distinctive dome-shaped Italian bunkers still surviving on Sicily, especially along the coast. The naval strongholds and ports such as Syracuse, Augusta, Palermo, and Messina have a profusion of these, though many have become overgrown since the war or absorbed into new construction. In view of the relative lack of memorials and museums, a useful guide is the ever-dependable "After the Battle" magazine, which devoted an issue to Operation *Husky* (Number 77, 1992). A few artifacts have survived outside Sicily. The Ordnance Museum at Aberdeen Proving Ground for many years displayed three vehicles captured on Sicily, a Renault R-35 of 5ª compagnia, 102° Battalione carri, a Semovente 47/37 from an unidentified battalion, and a Semovente 90/53 from 10° Raggruppamento Semoventi.

There are numerous memorials to the 1943 campaign scattered around Sicily. Here, Lt. Cdr. Joaquin Correia from the US Naval Air Station Sigonella and Dr Giuseppe Abbate from the Gela Kiwanis Club take part in a wreath-laying ceremony at the memorial at Ponte Dirillo on July 9, 2009, the 66th anniversary of the invasion. This memorial is located at the base of the Biazza ridge; the photo of the Ponte Dirillo defenses shown earlier in this book are still located in the hills above. (US Navy)

FURTHER READING

Operation *Husky* has been well covered over the years. From the Allied side, there are superb official histories by the British, US, and Canadian armies, as well as accounts by the Royal Navy, US Navy, and US Army Air Force. Many of these histories were written in the 1950s and so the vital issue of Allied Ultra signals intelligence was not openly discussed. Fortunately, the superb Hinsley study has a chapter devoted to this subject. Besides the published studies, there are numerous specialized reports and monographs, many unpublished, covering the campaign. From the Axis side, the Italian perspective is covered by an account by Guzzoni's deputy, Gen. Faldella, as well as Santoni's more recent official history. The US National Archives and Records Administration in College Park, MD (NARA II) has an extensive collection of captured Italian army documents, including excellent order-of-battle data on Italian dispositions on Sicily. There is no official German account, though there are a variety of accounts contained within the US Army's Foreign Military Studies series by German commanders. Several of these were collected under the omnibus T-2 study. The most detailed English-language account of the Axis forces on Sicily was prepared under the direction of Magna Bauer to support the US Army's official "Green Book" history of *Husky*. The Bauer study consists of 18 separate reports in the R-114 to R-147 series, totaling over a thousand pages. It has not been published but it is available at NARA II. Dozens, if not hundreds, of divisional and other unit histories from formations participating in Operation *Husky* have appeared in print, but they are not listed here owing to their sheer volume.

Government reports
Bauer, Magna, *Axis Tactical Operations in Sicily, July–August 1943* (US Army Office of Chief of Military History: 1959)
Fries, Walter, et al., *The Battle of Sicily* (US Army Foreign Military Studies T-2: 1950)
Rodt, Eberhardt, *Studie über den Feldzug in Sizilien bei der 15. Pz.Gren.Div. Mai–August 1943* (US Army Foreign Military Studies C-077: 1950)
Westphal, Siegfried, et al., *The Italian Campaign April 1943–11 May 1944* (US Army Foreign Military Studies T-1A: 1950)
Airborne Missions in the Mediterranean 1942–1945 (USAF Historical Studies No. 74: 1955)
G-2 Estimate of the Enemy Situation (AFHQ: 1943)
Lessons from the Sicilian Campaign (AFHQ: 1943)
Notes on the Planning and Assault Phases of the Sicilian Campaign (Combined Operations Headquarters: 1943)
Participation of the Ninth & Twelfth Air Forces in the Sicilian Campaign (USAAF Historical Studies No. 37: 1945)
The Reduction of Pantelleria and Adjacent Islands 8 May–14 June 1943 (USAAF Historical Studies No. 52: 1945)
Report of the Operations of the US Seventh Army in the Sicilian Campaign 10 July–17 August 1943 (Seventh Army: 1943)
RAF Mediterranean Review, No. 4 July–September 1943 (HQ RAF: 1943)
The Sicilian Campaign 10 July–17 August 1943 (US Office of Naval Intelligence: 1945)

Books
Arena, Nino, *L'Italia in guerra 1940–45: Retroscena tecnico della disfatta* (Ermanno Albertelli: 1997)
Blackwell, Ian, *Battle for Sicily: Stepping Stone to Victory* (Pen & Sword: 2008)
Bragadin, Marc, *The Italian Navy in World War II* (US Naval Institute: 1957)
Breuer, Aiilaim, *Drop Zone Sicily: Allied Airborne Strike July 1943* (Presidio: 1943)
Clerici, Carlo, *Le difese costiere italiane nelle due guerre mondiali* (Storia Militare: 1996)
Craven, W. F. & Cate, J. L., *The Army Air Forces in World War II, Volume Two, Europe: Torch to Pointblank August 1942 to December 1943* (Office of Air Force History: 1983)
Deakin, F. W., *The Brutal Friendship: Mussolini, Hitler and the Fall of Italian Fascism* (Harper & Row: 1962)
Donato, Armando, *Messina Obiettive Strategico: Organizzazione difensiva ed eventi bellici 1940–1943* (EDAS: 2009)
D'Este, Carlo, *Bitter Victory: The Battle for Sicily 1943* (Collins: 1988)
Faldella, Emilio, *Lo sbarco e la difesa della Sicilia* (L'Ariene: 1956)
Ford, Ken, *Assault on Sicily: Monty and Patton at War* (Sutton: 2007)

Garland, Albert & Smyth, Howard, *Sicily and the Surrender of Italy* (US Army Center of Military History: 1965)

Greene, Jack & Massignani, Alessandro, *The Naval War in the Mediterranean 1940–43* (Chatham: 2002)

Hinsley, F. H., et al., *British Intelligence in the Second World War, Vol. 3, Part 1* (HMSO: 1984)

Marcon, Tullio, *Cento anni di Marina: Storia della Base Navale di Augusta e della Piazzaforte Augusta-Siracusa* (Ediprint: 1996)

Mitcham, Samuel & von Stauffenberg, Friedrich, *The Battle for Sicily: How the Allies Lost their Chance for Total Victory* (Orion: 1991)

Molony, C. J. C., et al., *History of the Second World War: The Mediterranean and Middle East, Volume V* (HMSO: 1973)

Morrison, Samuel, *History of the US Naval Operations in World War II: Sicily–Salerno–Anzio, Volume 9* (Little, Brown: 1954)

Nicholson, G. W. L., *Official History of the Canadian Army in the Second World War, Vol. II, The Canadians in Italy 1943–1945* (Queen's Printer: 1956)

Roskill, S. W., *The War at Sea 1939–1945, Volume III The Offensive, Part 1: 1 June 1943–31 May 1944* (HMSO: 1960)

Santoni, Alberto, *Le operazioni in Sicilia e in Calabria Luglio–Settembre 1943* (Stato Maggiore dell'Esercito: 1989)

von Senger und Etterlin, Frido, *Neither Fear nor Hope* (Macdonald: 1963)

Zuehlke, Mark, *Operation Husky: The Canadian Invasion of Sicily July 10–August 7, 1943* (Douglas and McIntyre: 2008)

INDEX